Multi-Sensory Parables

15 ready-to-use sessions on the stories Jesus told
– for creative churches and small groups

Ian Birkinshaw

MULTI-SENSORY PARABLES by Ian Birkinshaw
Scripture Union, 207–209 Queensway, Bletchley, MK2 2EB, UK
e-mail: info@scriptureunion.org.uk
www.scriptureunion.org.uk

Scripture Union Australia: Locked Bag 2, Central Coast Business Centre, NSW 2252
www.su.org.au

ISBN   978 1 84427 231 0

First published in Great Britain by Scripture Union 2006

Scripture quotations taken from the HOLY BIBLE, NEW INTERNATIONAL VERSION, NIV, © 1973, 1978, 1984 by International Bible Society. Used by permission of Hodder & Stoughton, a division of Hodder Headline Ltd. All rights reserved.

British Library Cataloguing-in-Publication data: a catalogue record for this book is available from the British Library.

Cover design by waldonwhitejones of Basildon, Essex, UK

Internal illustrations by Fred Chevalier and Helen Gale

Internal page design by Creative Pages: www.creativepages.co.uk

Printed and bound by Henry Ling Limited, at the Dorset Press, Dorchester, DT1 1HD.

Scripture Union is an international Christian charity working with churches in more than 130 countries providing resources to bring the good news about Jesus Christ to children, young people and families – and to encourage them to develop spiritually through the Bible and prayer. As well as coordinating a network of volunteers, staff and associates who run holidays, church-based events and school Christian groups, Scripture Union produces a wide range of publications and supports those who use their resources through training programmes.

Contents

For
George, Barbara, June, Alan and Vera

Thanks

Thanks to the people of St Michael le Belfrey, especially those who have supported the writing of this book through their prayers. Thanks to Ang Bryan, our cells coordinator, an exceptional co-leader, colleague and friend. Thanks to the members of my cell group (with apologies for my terrible coffee and the unreliable CD player), and to the members of the St Michael's Family Service planning team whose creativity and invention is a perpetual source of delight. Thanks to Riding Lights Theatre Company, the staff, actors, and students of the Summer Theatre School who have been the first to try out so many of these ideas. Thanks to Lin Ball at Scripture Union. Above all, I want to thank my wife Adele, and our children Peter and Sarah, for their unremitting encouragement, patience, loyalty, love and laughter.

Now to him who is able to do immeasurably more than all we ask or imagine, according to his power that is at work within us, to him be glory in the church and in Christ Jesus throughout all generations, for ever and ever! Amen.

Making the most of Multi-Sensory Parables

It's a fact – vibrant small groups make for strong disciples and growing churches! Two vital ingredients in sustaining a healthy small group are a balanced 'menu' and committed leadership.

A balanced menu

Have you ever been part of a small group that set out full of enthusiasm and great expectations, and yet before long the life had ebbed away? Some groups get hijacked by the concerns of one or two needy members; some degenerate into worthy but rather dreary Bible study; some groups slide to become cosy social gatherings. Pastoral care, prayer, Bible study, loving relationships – they're all important. But the challenge is to keep them in balance. *Multi-Sensory Parables* aims to provide lively and interactive Bible-based sessions that will put Christ at the centre, deepen fellowship and help your group turn faith into action.

The 15 sessions in *Multi-Sensory Parables* are built around a common 'menu' approach:

 ## Getting connected (allow 10–15 minutes)

This ice-breaker will get everyone involved and sharing together from the very beginning. It is easy to see the value of this part of a session when a group is just starting out or when new people have recently joined, but even if you have known each other for a long time you will often be surprised at what you discover.

 ## Touching God (allow 15–20 minutes)

Jesus encouraged his followers to engage with God through all their senses. For example:

> **Look** at the birds of the air – Matthew 6:26.
> My sheep **listen** to my voice – John 10:27.
> **Touch** me and see – Luke 24:39.
> Take and **eat**; this is my body – Matthew 26:26.
> She has done a beautiful thing (when Mary poured sweet-**smelling** perfume over Jesus) – Mark 14:6.

A small group is the ideal context for exploring multi-sensory worship.

 ## Living Scripture (allow 40–45 minutes)

The aim is to search the Scriptures, but also to allow the Scriptures to search us. 'All Scripture is God-breathed and is useful for teaching, rebuking, correcting and training in righteousness' (2 Timothy 3:16). Come expecting to be encouraged, challenged, changed.

The Living Scripture questions are based on the NIV (New International Version), but try reading the passage from an alternative version sometimes. Different voices will help bring the text to life, so experiment by having several people read the various characters, or try acting out the parables from time to time. Take a few moments to pray that God will inspire your discussion before you consider the questions.

Sometimes **Touching God** comes before **Living Scripture**, and sometimes afterwards as a response.

Reaching out (allow 15–20 minutes)

It is easy to skip over this part of the meeting, particularly if you have let an earlier section run on too long. A group that stops looking outwards will soon become stagnant. **Reaching out** often includes an idea for a social activity as a great way of drawing new people into the group. Plan one into your programme from time to time.

 ## Digging deeper

Suggestions for further exploration. The bookmarks can be copied and given out to group members to take home.

Leading a group

Some people shy away from leadership because they feel they do not know enough about the Bible, but a good small group leader is more likely to have pastoral gifts than an expert knowledge of Scripture. Here are a few pointers towards effective leadership. For more help, see Mike Law's excellent book *Small Groups Growing Churches,* Scripture Union, 2003.

Prepare well

Each of the sessions in *Multi-Sensory Parables* includes a choice of material. Look ahead and decide which of the suggestions are right for your group. Many of the ideas require some advance preparation. Have everything ready before people arrive so you can concentrate on making them welcome. Don't be afraid to use the material as a springboard for your own ideas. Add your own touches; mix and match activities to suit the particular needs of your group.

Pass it on

Sharing out responsibility for different parts of the meeting will strengthen the group. Work towards a rota where different people lead different sections each time. Meet in various homes so that everyone has the opportunity to practise hospitality (Romans 12:13). Appoint an assistant leader and let them run the meeting from time to time. If the group becomes too big to fit into one home, your assistant can start up a second group.

People-minded

Be people-focused rather than programme-driven. Hospitality is important. Timing is also important – start promptly and don't overrun. If you go on too late, people might think twice about coming back next time. Be aware of the quieter members and draw them in with a simple but direct question sometimes (eg 'Chris, what do you think?'). But be sensitive. If someone does not turn up, get in touch before the next meeting. The aim is not to pressurise people, but to let them know they matter.

Pray

Pray regularly – daily if possible – for the members of your group.

Finally

Finally, many of the ideas in *Multi-Sensory Parables* have been used effectively in all sorts of gatherings, large and small. You'll find most can be adapted for school assemblies, retreats, quiet days, camps, conferences, training events, church services, prayer meetings, etc. Step out and experiment. Let your imagination fly!

1 Arable parable

Mark 4:1–20

The parable of the sower

Jesus took his stories from the world around him: a world of peasant farmers and fishermen, of vineyards and village life. Here he describes a farmer out in the fields, sowing seed. There were two ways to get the job done. The farmer could scatter the seed by hand, or he could opt for a more 'hi-tech' approach: laying the sack of grain across the back of a donkey, making a hole in the bag, and leading the animal up and down the field. Either way, a proportion of the seed would inevitably fall on unproductive ground. The parable of the sower is partly a parable about parables: the people crowd around, hungry to hear the stories Jesus has to tell, but will his words take root in their hearts?

Afterwards, away from the hubbub, Jesus and his disciples chew over the story. They have been together for just a few weeks, but already the little band of followers have encountered opposition; they have heard Jesus denounced as a blasphemer and a lawbreaker (Mark 2:7,24), a madman and a magician (3:21,22). But Jesus urges them: don't lose heart! Remember the end of the story: 'Others, like seed sown on good soil, hear the word, accept it, and produce a crop – thirty, sixty or even a hundred times what was sown' (verse 20).

 Getting connected

Either

Secret messages
You will need: copies of the puzzles on page 11.

Divide the group into pairs and give each pair a copy of the puzzles. Alternatively, cut up a single copy of the sheet before the meeting and stick the ten puzzles around the room. Explain that each one represents a New Testament parable or saying. Allow 5-10 minutes for group members to identify the secret messages. When time is up, compare your answers (page 10).

Or

Down on the farm
Q: Have you ever spent time on a farm? What was it like? Share your experiences.

 Touching God

Either

Soil meditation
You will need: a polythene sheet to protect the floor; a bowl or bucket containing potting compost; a second bowl or bucket containing warm water; soap and towels; background music (optional).

Encourage everyone to plunge their hands into the potting compost and get them dirty! Invite people to get comfortable, perhaps holding their hands in their laps. When everyone is ready, read the meditation on page 13. (Don't read out the Scripture references – they are included for information.) Take it slowly and pause at the end of each section for people to pray in silence. You may like to play some gentle instrumental music in the background.

Or

Van Gogh

You will need: copies of the painting *Sower with Setting Sun* by Vincent van Gogh. Van Gogh produced more than 30 paintings inspired by the parable of the sower, and often incorporated the sun into his pictures as a symbol for Christ. Search the Internet for the version painted in Arles in 1888 and now displayed in the Rijksmuseum Krueller-Mueller, Otterlo.

Make sure everyone can see a copy of the painting. Allow four or five minutes for people to look at the picture and then share any observations or insights. Let your conversation lead you into prayer.

 Living Scripture – Mark 4:1–20

You will need: copies of the illustration of four types of soil on page 12; five volunteers to read the passage; five slips of paper to say which verses they should read:

Reader 1 (narrator): verses 1–3 and verses 9–14
Reader 2 (the path): verse 4 and verse 15
Reader 3 (rocky places): verses 5,6 and verses 16,17
Reader 4 (thorns): verse 7 and verses 18,19
Reader 5 (good soil): verse 8 and verse 20

Give everyone a copy of the soil pictures to look at as they listen to the parable being read. Then discuss the questions.

1   What do the following represent in the parable: the farmer; the seed; the soil? The harvest in verse 20 is often interpreted to mean new converts to the Christian faith. Could it also be understood in other ways?

2   Looking at verses 15–19, make a list of the things which block understanding and spoil growth. How have you experienced these in your own life?

3   Why did Jesus teach through parables instead of stating things plainly? (You may want to compare verses 10–12 with the longer explanation in Matthew 13:10–17.)

4   Jesus has called us to be partners with him in 'sowing the word'. What do you find in the passage to encourage you in this task?

5   Look again at the illustration of the four types of soil. Which one reminds you most of yourself right now? Take a minute in silence to reflect, then break into pairs or threes and pray for each other.

 **Reaching out**

Either

Sowers, reapers, growers

You will need: Post-it notes; three sheets of paper: one brown, one yellow, one green; Blu-tack; marker pens.

Write the word SOWERS on the brown sheet of paper, REAPERS on the yellow, and GROWERS on the green. Stick these up on the wall. Give each member of the group a Post-it note and ask them to write their own name on it. Then explain:

God calls us to work together in the task of sowing, reaping and growing.

— *Sowers* enjoy meeting new people and building friendships.

— *Reapers* are good at explaining the gospel and talking about their personal experience of Jesus Christ. They are good at helping people over the threshold of faith.

— *Growers* are good at supporting new Christians and encouraging spiritual growth.

Decide together who are the sowers, reapers and growers in your group. Stick your Post-it notes on the appropriate sheet. Pray as a group for opportunities to use your gifts.

Or

Indoor gardening

You will need: four or five miniature daffodil or other spring flowering bulbs; a plant pot; some potting compost; coarse sand or gravel; a garden trowel or large spoon.

This is an activity for the autumn. Plant the bulbs and arrange for a member of the group to take them as a gift to someone you know who is in need of encouragement. You may also like to attach a card with a suitable verse or prayer.

To plant your bulbs:

Put a layer of gritty sand or gravel in the bottom of the plant pot. Cover the gravel with potting compost until the pot is about half full. Do not firm the mixture down at this stage. Press the bulbs gently into the soil. Make sure the bulbs are not touching each other or the sides of the pot. Fill the pot to within 2.5 cm of the rim to allow space for watering.

Digging deeper

Give each member of the group a copy of bookmark 1 on page 74 to take home.

Answers:

1 No one puts a lamp under a bowl (Matthew 5:15)

2 A false prophet is like a wolf in sheep's clothing (Matthew 7:15)

3 Parable of the wise and foolish builders (Matthew 7:24–27)

4 Parable of the ten bridesmaids (Matthew 25:1–13)

5 Separating the sheep from the goats (Matthew 25:31–33)

6 Parable of the growing seed (Mark 4:26–29)

7 Parable of the friend at midnight (Luke 11:5–8)

8 Parable of the rich fool (Luke 12:16–21)

9 Parable of the lost son (Luke 15:11–32)

10 Parable of the persistent widow (Luke 18:1–8)

SECRET MESSAGE

BOWL ~~LAMP~~

SECRET MESSAGE

wowolfol

SECRET MESSAGE

YYYY
+ foolish
builders

SECRET MESSAGE

bridesmaid bridesmaid
bridesmaid bridesmaid
bridesmaid bridesmaid
bridesmaid bridesmaid
bridesmaid bridesmaid

SECRET MESSAGE

EWE
RAM

BILLY
NANNY

SECRET MESSAGE

sEE D

SECRET MESSAGE

NIG*buddy*HT

SECRET MESSAGE

FOO£

SECRET MESSAGE

MISSING PER ✳ ✳ ✳

SECRET MESSAGE

WIDOW
WIDOW
WIDOW
WIDOW
WIDOW

Arable parable

Firm foundations

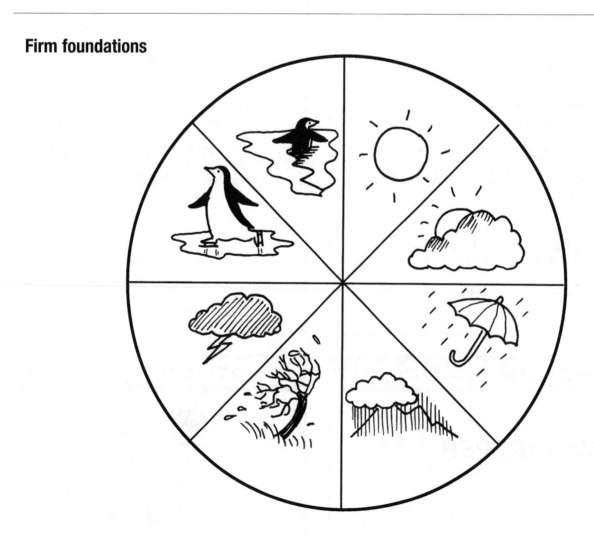

Soil meditation

Look at your hands. How do they feel? Are you used to getting your hands dirty? Perhaps you work with soil, or dig your garden for recreation. Maybe the sensation of earth in the creases of your skin is familiar and friendly. Or maybe the dirt feels like it doesn't belong, and you can't wait to get clean. Smell the soil. Does it have a smell...?

Hear these words from the Bible: 'First this: God created the Heavens and Earth – all you see, all you don't see ... God formed Man out of dirt from the ground and blew into his nostrils the breath of life. The Man came alive – a living soul! Then God planted a garden in Eden, in the east. He put the Man he had just made in it. God made all kinds of trees grow from the ground, trees beautiful to look at and good to eat.' (*The Message*: Genesis 1:1; 2:7–9)

Dirt – rich, dark earth – full of the promise of life. Look at the dirt on your hands, and in the quiet of your own heart thank God for the gift of life...

One word for soil is 'humus'. From it, we get the word 'humility'. Humility is about knowing our beginnings, keeping our feet on the ground, knowing that we're nothing without the breath of God within us. But sometimes we lose touch with reality. The Scriptures encourage us to 'Humble yourselves before the Lord, and he will lift you up' (James 4:6,10). But so often, pride and selfishness muddy our lives...

Jesus Christ was one with God, and yet – for our sake – he humbled himself and became a person like us. His blood ran and mingled with the soil; his broken body was hidden in the ground. Jesus bit the dust, so we could be clean.

If you're aware of some sin that soils your life, make these words from a psalm your own prayer: 'Have mercy on me, O God, according to your unfailing love ... Wash away all my iniquity and cleanse me from my sin' (Psalm 51:1,2)...

'As he went along, Jesus saw a man blind from birth ... he spat on the ground, made some mud with the saliva, and put it on the man's eyes. "Go," he told him, "wash in the Pool of Siloam" ... So the man went and washed, and came home seeing' (John 9:1,6,7). Jesus used dirt to heal a man who couldn't see. He daubed it on his body, and sent him to wash. In a few moments, we're going to wash our hands. Is there some healing work you want Jesus to accomplish in you? Or perhaps there's some perplexing situation and you can't see the way forward. Tell him about it now...

Here's a poem written by George Herbert (*Trinity Sunday*):

> *Lord, who hast formed me out of mud,*
> *And hast redeemed me through thy blood,*
> *And sanctified me to do good;*
> *Purge all my sins done heretofore:*
> *For I confess my heavy score,*
> *And I will strive to sin no more.*
> *Enrich my heart, mouth, hands in me,*
> *With faith, with hope, with charity;*
> *That I may run, rise, rest with thee.*

In your own time, when you're ready, and without breaking the silence, let's wash.

2 Firm foundations

Matthew 7:24–29

The parable of the wise and foolish builders

Jesus had first-hand experience of the construction industry. As a carpenter, he must have known all about the importance of building a house on solid foundations. He would also have been familiar with the hazardous local terrain. The crowd probably roared with laughter at the antics of the lazy and unwary builder, fooled into thinking a parched river bed was the ideal site for a new house. During the hot summer months many rivers dried up, but everyone knew that in the winter the sandy hollow would once again become a raging watercourse.

The parable of the wise and foolish builders comes at the very end of Jesus' Sermon on the Mount (Matthew 5–7). Throughout this discourse he urges his listeners to explore a radical new way of life based on purity of heart and self-giving love. The parable is his parting shot: he has not come to offer a charming philosophy – Christ himself is the only sure foundation.

 ## Getting connected

Either

Tabloid towers
You will need: old newspapers; two rolls of sticky tape; two pairs of scissors.

Divide into two teams. Give each team a supply of old newspapers, sticky tape and a pair of scissors. Compete to see who can build the tallest free-standing tower using rolled up newspaper. Allow about 10 minutes.

Or

Location, location, location
Q: If you were going to build an idyllic holiday hideaway, would you choose a remote mountain setting, a secluded beach, or some other location? Why? Share your thoughts with the group.

 ## Touching God

Either

Toolbox prayers
You will need: a large box containing an assortment of tools and DIY materials. Make sure it contains a wide variety of items – for example, hammer and nails, Stanley knife, hacksaw, trowel, torch, tape measure, plumb line, spirit level, sandpaper, electrical plug, light switch, paintbrush, copper piping, an old tap, blowlamp, lock and key, wallpaper, wood, wire, glue, string.

Invite each person to select an item from the box. When everyone has made their choice ask them to reflect in silence on ways in which the object reminds them of Jesus Christ. For example, a hammer is a reminder that Jesus was nailed to the cross to save us from our sins; a tape measure is a reminder of 'how wide and long and high and deep is the love of Christ' (Ephesians 3:18).

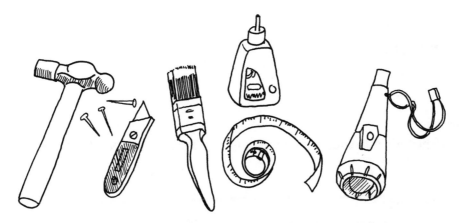

Allow two or three minutes for reflection, then share your thoughts and let them lead you into prayer and praise.

Or

Foundation stones

You will need: an assortment of small pebbles, the more colourful the better; background music (optional); seven slips of paper prepared with the following references: (1) Job 38:4–7; (2) Proverbs 3:19,20; (3) Psalm 89:14; (4) Isaiah 33:5,6; (5) Isaiah 28:16; (6) Ephesians 2:19,20; (7) 1 Corinthians 3:11.

Give each member of the group seven pebbles. Ask for volunteers to read the passages and hand out the slips of paper. If the group has fewer than seven members, some will need to read more than once. You may like to play a piece of quiet instrumental music as a background to the activity.

When everyone is ready, the first volunteer reads out Job 38:4–7. Pause for a moment. The reader then places a pebble on the ground and everyone takes it in turns to add a stone, working together in silence to build up the shape of a cross. Then the second volunteer reads Proverbs 3:19,20 and everyone adds a second pebble. Continue in this way, extending and enlarging the cross until you have heard all seven readings.

Keep silent for a few moments and look at what you have made. Let what you see, and the words you have heard, lead you into prayer and praise.

 Living Scripture – Matthew 7:24–29

You will need: copies of the weather chart on page 12.

1   What do the following represent in the parable: the houses (verses 24,26), the storm (verses 25,27), the rock (verses 24,25), the sand (verse 26)?

2   The two houses are put to the test when the storms come. What does this parable say to anyone who thinks that the Christian faith guarantees a trouble free life?

3   Read Ephesians 2:8–10 and James 2:14–18. If we are saved through faith and not through good works, why is it so important to put Jesus' words into practice (verse 24)?

4   Which of Jesus' commands do you find it hard to keep?

5   Give everyone a copy of the weather chart. What sort of 'weather conditions' are you experiencing in your life right now? Break into pairs or threes to discuss the symbols you have chosen and pray for each other.

Reaching out

Either

Historic building
Plan a visit to an historic building. Invite guests from outside the group to join you.

Or

DIY or decorating party
Do you know anyone who would appreciate help with DIY or decorating? Could the group offer to lend a hand? Decide who will make contact.

Or

Sure foundation
Which of your friends or family members would you love to introduce to Jesus Christ to become the foundation of their lives? Take a few moments in quiet and pray that the Holy Spirit will bring people to mind. Come back together and make a list of any names you have thought of. Pray for them now, and continue to pray for them in future meetings.

 Digging deeper

Give each member of the group a copy of bookmark 2 on page 74 to take home.

3 Finders keepers

Matthew 13:44–46

The parables of the hidden treasure and the pearl

In a world without High Street banks, the only way most people had of protecting their belongings was to hide them in the ground. In the first of these two snapshots, a man stumbles across a fantastic hoard of treasure, buried for safe keeping and then forgotten. Rabbinic law was clear – 'Finders, keepers!' – so he sells all he has in order to possess the field. The second snapshot concerns a dealer searching for fine pearls. Pearls were highly prized; Cleopatra is said to have owned one worth 25 million denarii. When the dealer finds a pearl of unsurpassable beauty, he gives everything to acquire it.

Both parables make the same point: though it comes at a price, there is no joy to compare with the kingdom of heaven. '… I have suffered the loss of all things, and do count them but dung, that I may win Christ, and be found in him!' (Philippians 3:8 – *Authorised Version*).

 Getting connected

Diamond heist

You will need: the Wallace and Gromit movie *The Wrong Trousers* on DVD or video (optional).

If possible, introduce the question below with the scene from *The Wrong Trousers* where Feathers McGraw steals the diamond from the museum. Begin with Wallace climbing onto the roof, and stop when they make their escape into the street. The sequence (entitled *Diamond Heist* on the DVD) lasts about 5 minutes.

Q: What 'treasure' (eg a precious object, a relationship, a job) cost you a lot of effort to acquire? What lengths did you go to, to get it? Was it worth it?

 Living Scripture – Matthew 13:44–46

1 The first man comes across the treasure by accident, but the merchant finds the pearl after a search. Which of the two parables is the best picture of your own encounter with Jesus Christ?

2 How is the kingdom of heaven like hidden treasure?

3 How does the first man react when he stumbles across the treasure? What does it cost him to acquire it? What is the message for anyone who wants to become a follower of Jesus?

4 What have you had to give up to follow Christ?

5 The pearl is usually taken to represent Christ, but the parable has also been understood as a picture of Christ (the merchant) searching for his Church (the pearl) – compare Luke 19:10. Which interpretation do you prefer? Are both equally valid?

 Touching God

Either

Greater gifts than gold

You will need: yellow play dough; clean scrap paper; background music (optional).

> ### Recipe for play dough
>
> You will need: 2 cups plain flour; 1 cup salt; 2 tablespoons oil; 2 tablespoons cream of tartar; 2 cups cold water; yellow food colouring.
>
> Mix all the ingredients in a pan and cook on a low heat until the dough reaches the required consistency. Knead thoroughly and allow to cool.
>
> You can prepare your dough several days in advance and store it in an airtight container.

Give everyone a lump of dough and a sheet of scrap paper to work on. Encourage them to create a sculpture representing something for which they want to thank God. You may want to play background music while you work. Allow 5–10 minutes, then gather your 'treasures' together and share the stories behind what you have made. Finish by praying together or singing a hymn of praise.

Or

Greater gifts than gold/alternative

You will need: photocopies of the treasure map on page 19, coloured pencils or pens. Instead of using play dough, ask everyone to draw their 'treasure' on the map, and then share it with one or two others.

 ## Reaching out

Either

Treasure hunt

Plan a social event where teams follow a trail of clues (on foot or in cars) to find hidden treasure. There could be challenges, questions or puzzles to be solved along the way, or items which have to be collected. Invite guests from outside the group to join you. Send people out at five-minute intervals or devise different routes so the teams cannot cheat by following one another! Gather for a drink in a home or local pub at the end of your quest.

Or

Prayer beads

You will need: a selection of attractive beads; lengths of coloured string.

'The kingdom of heaven is like treasure hidden in a field' (verse 44). Pray together for friends or family members who have yet to discover this treasure for themselves. Encourage everyone to choose a bead to represent each person they pray for. Thread them onto the string to make bracelets or key fobs as a reminder to go on praying.

 ## Digging deeper

Give each member of the group a copy of bookmark 3 on page 74 to take home.

Greater gifts than gold

4 Pass it on

Matthew 18:21–35

The parable of the unmerciful servant

'Lord, how many times shall I forgive someone who sins against me?' was the question Peter asked Jesus. Most rabbis said three times, taking the prophet Amos as their guide (Amos 1:3). Peter thought he was being generous when he suggested seven, but Jesus rejected any kind of tally. Instead, he tells a story about a servant who owes his king ten thousand bags of gold – a vast sum: 30 times more than all the taxes gathered in Galilee each year. The debt owed by the second servant is chicken feed by comparison – the equivalent of three months' wages.

The parable calls attention to the vital importance of forgiving. It is a spiritual dynamic Jesus has addressed before (Matthew 6:12,14,15). God's grace is like water flowing through a pond: if there is no outlet we will soon become stagnant and poisonous.

 Getting connected

Either

Receiving end

Q: Has anyone done a kind or generous thing for you this week? Discuss your experiences together.

Or

Pay off

Q: If someone suddenly offered to pay off all your debts, how would you celebrate?

Or

Keeper of the keys

You will need: a bunch of keys; a blindfold.

If you are meeting in a large room you might like to play this game. Place the bunch of keys under a chair in the centre of the group. Recruit a volunteer to be keeper of the keys. Have them sit on the chair and blindfold them. One by one, members of the group attempt to steal the keys. If the keeper of the keys hears anyone approaching, they must point in the direction of the sound. If the thief is caught, they return to their place empty-handed. A successful thief becomes the new keeper of the keys.

 Living Scripture – Matthew 18:21–35

You will need: a piece of string about 150 cm long, the ends tied to make a big loop; the set of 18 cards photocopied from page 23; a calculator (optional).

Use the string to make a circle in the centre of the group and share out the cards. Explain that these are all comments or sayings about forgiveness on which people may have different views. The first person reads their first card aloud. If they agree with the statement they place the card face up within the circle; if they do not agree, they place it outside the circle. Do not discuss or comment at this stage. Continue around the group, taking it in turns to read and respond, until all 18 statements have been considered. Now invite anyone who would like to change the position of any of the cards to give their reason. Try to come to a whole-group consensus.

Read the passage together and then tackle the questions.

1 What do the following represent in the parable: the king; the servants; the debts?

2 A silver coin (a denarius) was the daily wage for an ordinary working man. A bag of gold (a talent) was worth the equivalent of 6000 silver coins. How much would a present-day labourer earn for eight hours' work? Multiply your estimate by 100 and write down the answer. Multiply the same estimate by 6000, then again by 10,000 and write down the new amount. What do you think Jesus meant to convey by these figures?

3 Why do you think the first servant refused to pardon his fellow-servant, even though the king had been so generous to him? How might unforgiveness be like being a prisoner?

4 How does the parable answer Peter's question in verse 21? What spiritual principles does the parable reveal?

5 In the light of your discussion, do you want to revise any of the decisions you made about the cards?

 Touching God

Either

Release for the captives
You will need: an assortment of old keys, enough for one each; a rough cross made from two sticks tied together and fixed into a plant pot by surrounding with small stones; appropriate background music – perhaps a song or hymn celebrating the cross of Christ.

Stand the cross in the centre of the group. Clear away the cards you rejected during the **Living Scripture** activity and arrange the remaining statements around the cross. Give everyone a key.

Is there anyone you need to forgive? Sometimes we disregard the things that have hurt us, and they lie buried, disturbing our peace. Begin by asking the Holy Spirit to bring to mind any unresolved business. Play the background music and encourage everyone to hold the key in their hand as they pray in silence. Imagine turning the key in a prison door and releasing someone from their debt. If there is no one you need to forgive, thank God for sending Jesus to release you from your debt to him. Allow five minutes for reflection.

Now read out Matthew 18:18. Take it in turns to place your keys in the pot at the base of the cross. As you do so, encourage each person to repeat the words, 'Forgive us our sins, as we forgive those who sin against us.'

Finish by praying the Lord's Prayer together, or by singing a song which celebrates our freedom in Christ.

Or

Release for the captives/alternative version
You will need: strips of paper approximately 29 cm x 10 cm (preferably red or grey); a stapler; a rough cross; background music – perhaps a song or hymn celebrating the cross of Christ.

Instead of keys, give everyone a strip of paper and ask them to write down the name of anyone they need to forgive, or any personal sins they are struggling with. No one will see what has been written. When the time for reflection is finished, fold the paper lengthways so the writing is hidden inside. Now pass the stapler around the group and use it to turn your individual strips into a paper chain. Drape the completed chain around the cross and pray the Lord's Prayer together.

Read Matthew 18:18, then tear up the paper chain – encourage everyone to participate in this – and scatter the fragments around the cross.

 ## Reaching out

Welcome back
Make a list of the people who have stopped coming to your group or church during the last year. Do you know why they left? Some may have made a sudden break because of a difficult relationship or some other disappointment; others may simply have drifted away through busyness. How could you reach out and let them know they have not been forgotten – perhaps with a card, a phone call, a visit, or an invitation to coffee? Decide on a plan of action and pray for each person.

 ## Digging deeper

Give each member of the group a copy of bookmark 4 on page 74 to take home.

Pass it on – Forgiveness cards

To err is human, to forgive divine.

Revenge is sweet.

If we do not forgive others, God will not forgive us.

If we do not forgive others, God cannot forgive us.

To say, 'I forgive, but I cannot forget,' is another way of saying, 'I cannot forgive.'

Holding a grudge is like letting someone live rent free in your head.

Forgiveness is costly.

Forgiveness is like unlocking a door to set someone free and realising you were the prisoner.

Definition of hell: a world without forgiveness.

Forgiveness is healing.

Forgiveness is not fair.

Forgiving is a choice, not a feeling.

Forgive everyone's faults except your own.

Forgiveness begins when someone says sorry.

Forgiving someone means keeping no record of wrongs.

It is easier to forgive the people who never meant to hurt us.

Forgiveness feels like weakness.

The only thing harder than forgiving is *not* forgiving.

5 Love actually

Luke 10:25–37

The parable of the good Samaritan

The 17-mile stretch of road between Jerusalem and Jericho winds down through barren desert and craggy hill country. In places, the rocks are red in colour, but that is not the only reason why it has long been known as 'The Way of Blood'. For most of history it has been notorious as the haunt of thieves and muggers. Only a courageous or a reckless traveller would walk the route alone. This is the setting for the parable of the good Samaritan.

Jesus told his story in reply to an expert in the law who asked, 'Who is my neighbour?' (verse 29). When Jesus introduced the Samaritan, his audience would certainly have expected him to be the villain of the piece. Bitter conflict between the Jews and the Samaritans had rumbled on for hundreds of years. It came to a head during Jesus' lifetime when, one Passover (probably in the year AD 6), a pack of Samaritans crept into Jerusalem under cover of darkness and defiled the Temple courts by scattering human remains.

But, in Jesus' story, the enemy turns out to be a hero, and his care for the hapless traveller stands as a challenge to all of us who, when it comes to love, are strong on theory and weak in practice.

 Getting connected

Either

Day's journey

You will need: photocopies of about 20 assorted road signs. The Department of Transport allows copies to be made from *The Highway Code* booklet or from the website www.highwaycode.gov.uk/signs_index.htm for study use.

Signs that would be most useful include:

crossroads	two-way traffic	slippery road
one way	uneven road surface	hazard exclamation mark
Z bends	incline	stop sign
no left turn	hump-back bridge	pedestrians
no U-turn	70mph speed limit	overhead power lines
roundabout	road works	riverbank (car going over
no entry	falling rocks	edge)

Choose a road sign to describe your day. For example, if you encountered unexpected difficulties you might pick 'falling rocks'; if you had to make an important decision you might opt for 'crossroads'. Invite each group member to choose a sign and describe why they picked that one.

Or

Helping hand

Q: Has a stranger ever helped you out of a dangerous or difficult situation? Share your experiences.

 **Touching God**

Prayer stations

Set up a series of prayer stations based on the parable of the good Samaritan. If you have access to a garden and the weather is favourable, you might like to set them up outdoors. Choose from the suggestions on page 27. Photocopy the page and cut out each set of instructions.

Allow about 15 minutes for people to visit the various stations and follow the directions given. Some may want to spend a little time at each one, while others might choose to spend the whole time praying in one place.

You will need (in addition to the photocopied card for each station):

ROAD – a basket containing an assortment of stones;

ROBBER – a toy weapon, a basket containing palm crosses, or crosses cut from card;

BANDAGES – a large twig fixed upright in a plant pot by surrounding with small stones, a basket containing several short lengths of bandage;

OIL – a small dish of olive oil, tissues or a cloth for wiping fingers;

WINE – a glass of wine, a cloth or tissue for wiping the rim after drinking.

 Living Scripture – Luke 10:25–37

Recruit two volunteers to act out the scene between Jesus and the expert in the law. Begin where the lawyer stands to ask his question. It was the custom for a Jewish rabbi to sit when teaching, so the person playing Jesus should remain seated. Then answer the questions together.

1 'Teacher, what must I do to inherit eternal life?' (verse 25). What do you notice about Jesus' first response to the expert in the law (verse 26)?

2 Why do you think the priest (verse 31) and then the Levite (verse 32) decided not to get involved with the injured traveller? Read Leviticus 21:1–3. Did they have good reason for passing by on the other side of the road?

3 Why did Jesus make the hero of the story a Samaritan? If he were telling the story today, what would be a modern equivalent? Who are the outsiders and victims of prejudice in your local community?

4 What did the Samaritan sacrifice in order to help the injured man? Make a list.

5 'Who is my neighbour?' (verse 29). How would you sum up the lesson of the parable? What did Jesus mean when he said, 'Go and do likewise' (verse 37)?

6 How do you think the expert in the law would have felt after hearing the parable? How does the parable make you feel? Take two minutes in silence to reflect and then share your thoughts. You may want to break into pairs or threes to pray for each other.

Reaching out

Either

Victim support

How could you reach out to support outsiders and victims of prejudice in your local community? Decide on a plan of action.

Or

Care for the sick

Who do you know who is ill or injured at the moment? What practical help could you offer? For example, if you know someone recovering after a stay in hospital, perhaps the group could arrange to cook them a meal every day for a week.

 Digging deeper

Give each member of the group a copy of bookmark 5 on page 74 to take home.

Prayer stations

ROAD

A cairn is a pile of stones made by travellers to mark a place or an event. Pause here for a moment and give thanks to God for a prayer answered, or ask for help if you are facing a difficult situation. When you have finished, select a stone to represent your prayer and add it to the cairn.

ROBBER

'The thief comes only to steal and kill and destroy; I have come that they may have life, and have it to the full' (John 10:10). Is there something or someone that has been taken from you recently? Commit your loss to the Lord. Hold one of the crosses in your hand while you pray. When you have finished praying, take the cross with you.

BANDAGES

'He heals the broken-hearted and binds up their wounds' (Psalm 147:3). Pause to pray for anyone you know who is sick or injured. When you have finished, tie a piece of bandage to one of the branches of the tree before you continue on your way.

OIL

'I am the LORD, who heals you' (Exodus 15:26). Jesus taught his disciples to pray for the sick by anointing them with oil. If you are ill, ask a friend to stop and pray for you. Have them dip their fingertip into the oil and draw a cross on your forehead. As they do so, they could pray: 'I anoint you in the name of Christ. Receive his healing touch to make you whole.'

WINE

'This is my blood of the covenant, which is poured out for many for the forgiveness of sins' (Matthew 26:28). Pause to confess your sins to God and ask for his forgiveness. Take a sip of wine and remember Christ's death on the cross. Wipe the rim of the glass before you move on.

6 Breadtime story

Luke 11:1–13

The parable of the friend at midnight

This parable begins with a catering crisis. A friend has arrived, footsore and in need of a good meal, but the larder is bare. It is midnight – the whole village is silent and sleeping – but hospitality is a sacred duty, so the embarrassed host goes out into the night in search of bread.

Jesus told the story in response to a plea from his disciples: 'Lord, teach us to pray'. What follows is a prayer masterclass, and the opening word – 'Abba' ('Daddy') – sets the tone for the whole passage.

God is not a remote or reluctant giver, hiding behind a door on which is the sign, 'Do not disturb.' He is the God who neither slumbers nor sleeps (Psalm 121:4). He answers our prayers not to be rid of us, but because he loves us.

 ## Getting connected

Either

Catering calamity
Q: When did you last have a crisis in the kitchen? What happened? Share your experiences.

Or

Given and received
Q: Do you have anything with you that was given as a gift (perhaps a Bible, or a special pen, or an item of clothing)? Who gave it to you? Is there a story behind it? Share those stories.

 ## Touching God

Either

Bruce Almighty
You will need: a copy of the Jim Carrey movie *Bruce Almighty* on DVD or video.

Watch the sequence where Bruce is overwhelmed by people praying. Set the scene by reading the blurb from the DVD/video case, then play the clip from the end of the restaurant scene when Bruce first hears voices in his head (13 on the DVD). Stop at the party scene, and his line, 'Coach prays a lot.' The whole sequence lasts about six minutes.

In the group, talk about how God has answered your prayers recently.

Finally, pray together, thanking God for the gift of prayer.

Or

Lord's Prayer cards
You will need: a photocopied set of ten Lord's Prayer cards (page 31); a plate or basket containing three bread rolls; a candle or lantern; background music (optional).

Put the bread and the lit candle or lantern in the centre of the group. If you are meeting after dark, turn out the room lights and pray by candlelight. Share out the Lord's Prayer cards and pray together as follows: the first person reads the first line from the Lord's Prayer and everyone repeats it. The second person waits for five seconds so that everyone can briefly reflect on the words before reading the next line, and so on.

Living Scripture – Luke 11:1–13

Read the passage or, if you prefer, act out the parable: invite three volunteers to play the characters. Begin with a knock at the door and the line, 'Gracious! How lovely to see you! I wasn't expecting you.' Then improvise.

Afterwards, tackle the questions together:

1 What do you think it means to pray with 'boldness', 'persistence' or 'shameless audacity', as various translations describe it (verse 8)?

2 God is depicted as a father (verses 2,11–13) and a friend (verses 5–7). How do these images encourage you?

3 The Lord's Prayer is a community prayer ('us', 'our', 'we' – verses 3,4). Do you find it easier to pray with others or by yourself; for others or for yourself?

4 The Lord's Prayer is a model prayer. What different elements of prayer does Jesus include? Which of these elements take up most of your own prayer time? How would you like your prayer life to grow?

5 Why does Jesus conclude his tutorial on prayer by speaking about the Holy Spirit?

6 What gift do you need from your generous Father in heaven?

Divide into pairs to discuss the last question, then write a prayer for each other on a Post-it note and stick it on the door.

If you have bread rolls left over from the **Touching God** activity, break off a piece of bread to share with your partner.

Reaching out

Either

Current affairs
You will need: a copy of today's newspaper, or a short news bulletin pre-recorded from TV or radio.

Share out pages from the newspaper and allow 5–10 minutes while people read, or listen to the news broadcast together. Pray about the issues that arise.

Or

Rapid response
If your church doesn't already have one, set up a telephone prayer chain.

Start by drawing up a list of names and telephone numbers of people who are willing to pray when a need arises. The person organising the chain goes first on the list. Anyone requesting prayer should contact them. They pass on the details to the second person, the second person contacts the third, and so on. If someone is out, do not leave a message but move on to the next number.

Once the chain is established you could publicise it in your local community.

 Digging deeper

Give each member of the group a copy of bookmark 6 on page 75 to take home.

Lord's Prayer cards

1

Our Father in heaven …

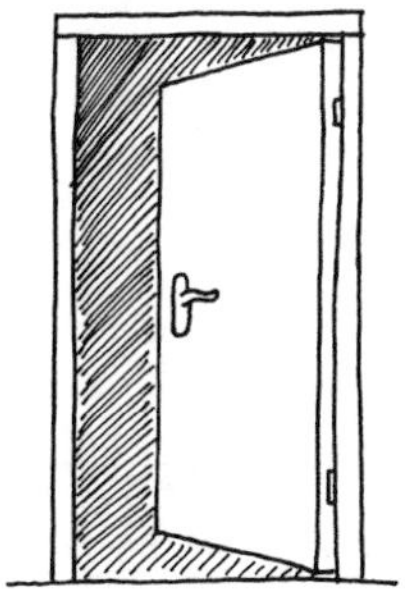

2

Hallowed be your name …

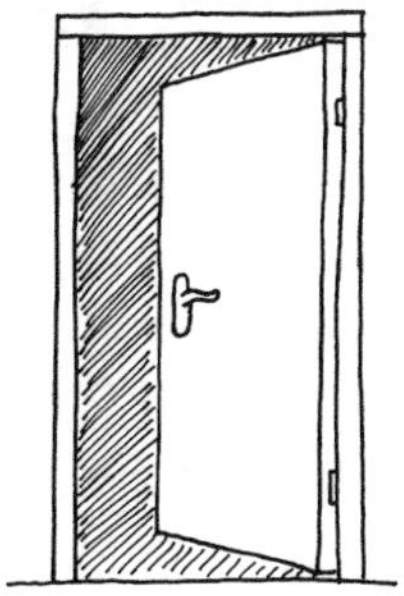

3

Your kingdom come, your will be done on earth as in heaven …

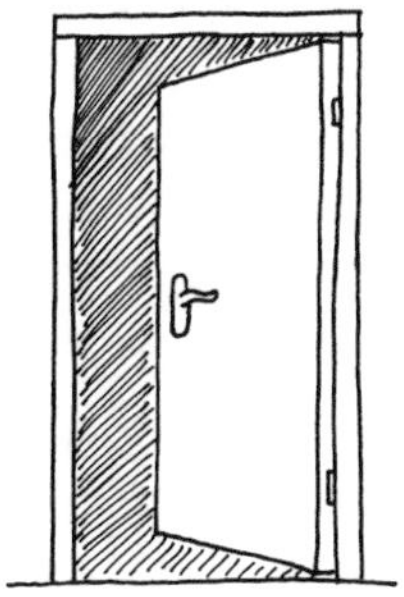

4

Give us today our daily bread …

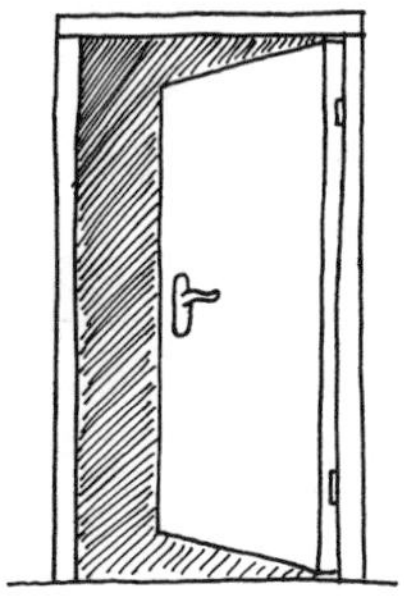

5

Forgive us our sins …

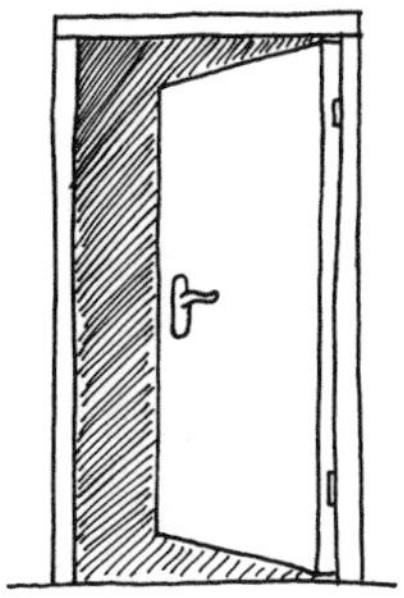

6

As we forgive those who sin against us …

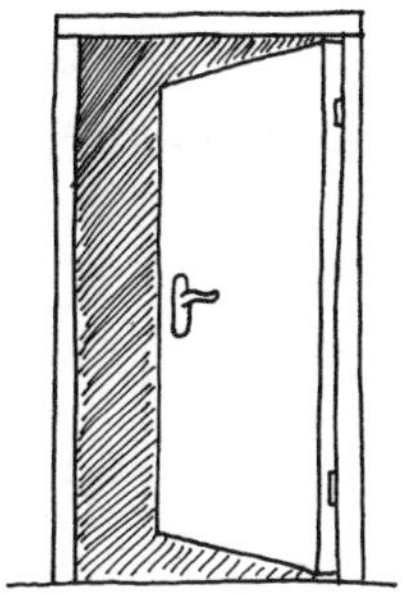

7

Lead us not into temptation …

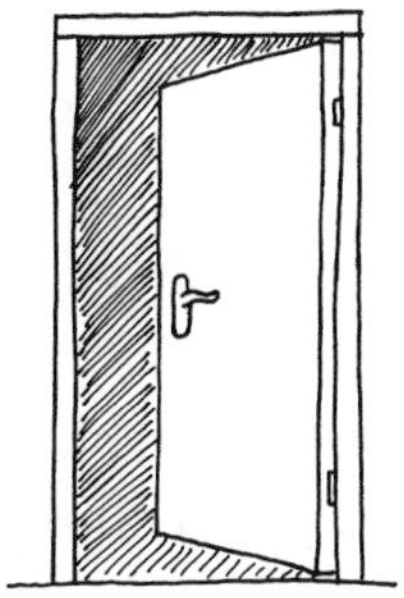

8

But deliver us from evil …

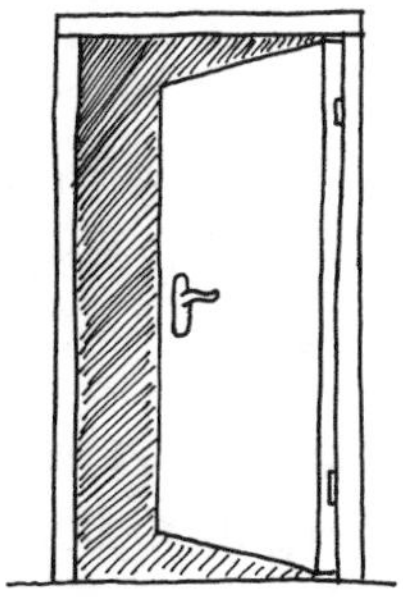

9

For the kingdom, the power, and the glory are yours …

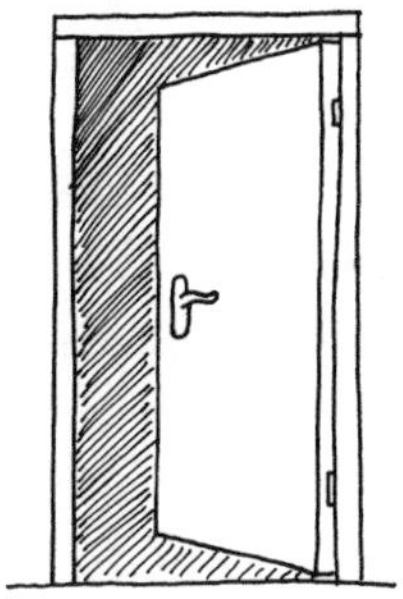

10

Now and for ever. Amen.

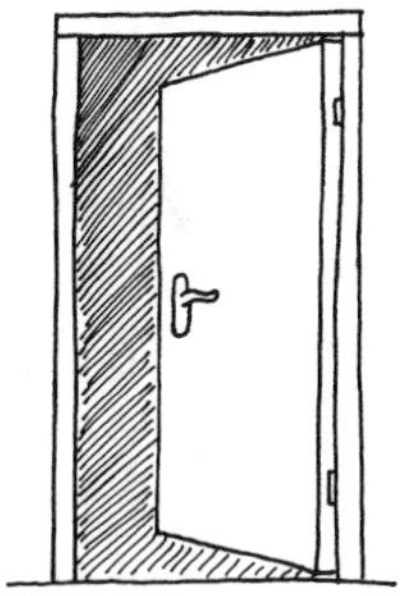

7 A fool and his money

Luke 12:13–34

The parable of the rich fool

It was customary for people to take their legal wrangles to a rabbi, but when a man asked Jesus to step in and settle a family dispute about money, he refused to get involved. Instead, he told a parable about a rich landowner whose priorities were dangerously skewed. The man in the story is like the fool in Psalm 14:1, trusting in worldly wealth and saying in his heart, 'There is no God.'

Fear and lack of faith entice us into living as though God's love is in short supply. Jesus urged his followers to consider the evidence and think again.

 Getting connected

Either

Eat, drink and be merry
You will need: *Jenga* game.

Set up the game according to the rules. Take it in turns to remove a block and replace it on top of the stack. Each time someone moves a block, they name a favourite food, drink, or leisure activity. Continue until the tower collapses.

Or

What's in store?
Q: Do you throw away things you no longer need, or keep them in case they come in useful? What sort of items do you hold on to? What do your cupboards say about you? Discuss in the group.

 Touching God

Pray it with flowers
You will need: a selection of different cut flowers, enough for everyone to have one each; a vase; background music (optional).

Let everyone choose a flower and place the empty vase in the centre of the group. Take a moment to get comfortable, then read the meditation on page 34. Don't hurry; pause where appropriate for people to reflect. You may want to play a piece of quiet instrumental music in the background, but make sure it is long enough to last throughout the whole meditation.

When you have finished praying, leave the vase of flowers in view.

 Living Scripture – Luke 12:13–34

You will need: a large bowl of water (use a large mixing bowl or fruit bowl); four or five paper petals for each person (see template on page 35).

1 Why do you think Jesus refused to get involved in the situation that prompted this parable (verses 13,14)?

2 The rich fool in Jesus' parable is a farmer. If you were going to turn the story into a contemporary television drama, who would your central character be? Think of a title for the drama that sums up the main point of the parable.

3 Has illness, hardship or bereavement ever made you rethink your priorities in life? How did you change?

4 What is the connection between greed (verse 15) and worry (verse 22)? What antidote does Jesus recommend (verses 24–34)?

5 'Provide purses for yourselves that will not wear out, a treasure in heaven that will not be exhausted ...' (verse 33). What might this mean in practice?

6 What do you worry about?

Take a few moments in quiet to reflect and write your responses to the last question on the paper petals. Invite people to talk about what they have written. Place the bowl of water in the centre of the group and pray together, asking God to help you worry less and trust him more. Encourage everyone to hold the petals in their hands while they pray, and then scatter them on the surface of the water as a sign that they are willing to release their worries to God.

 ## Reaching out

Either

Give to the poor
'Sell your possessions and give to the poor...' (verse 33). Give up a luxury you can live without for one week and send the money you save to a charity which supports the poor. For example, why not cycle to work and save the bus fare? Or give up your daily newspaper? Or make sandwiches instead of buying lunch? Or go without a trip to the cinema? Alternatively, clear out your cupboards and sell the things you no longer need at a car boot sale. Discuss the possibilities and make a list to remind yourselves what each member of the group has pledged to do.

Or

A problem shared
Who do you know who is weighed down by a particular worry at the moment? Pray for them. Arrange for a member of the group to call round with the bunch of flowers you used in the **Touching God** activity and let them know you have been thinking of them.

 ## Digging deeper

Give each member of the group a copy of bookmark 7 on page 75 to take home.

Pray it with flowers

Look closely at the flower in your hands… What attracted you to that particular one? Notice the shape … the way the different parts are connected. Let your fingers move gently over the stalk … the leaves … the petals … and experience the different textures…

Perhaps your flower has thorns; test them lightly against your fingertip to see how sharp they are… Which parts of the flower seem the most fragile; which parts are stronger? Carefully touch the centre, where the pollen is produced, and look at the fine yellow dust left behind on your finger.

What colour is your flower? What does that colour bring to mind? Now look again, a little more closely. How many different shades and colours do you really see? Could you name them all?

Smell your flower. Does it have a scent? Is it pleasant … unpleasant?

Imagine what it would be like to be this flower growing in a field or a garden. You have no control over the place where you exist, or the quality of the soil … or whether your face is turned towards the sun or the storm.

Jesus once told his friends, 'Consider how the lilies grow. They do not labour or spin. Yet I tell you, not even Solomon in all his splendour was dressed like one of these. If that is how God clothes the grass of the field, which is here today and tomorrow is thrown into the fire, how much more will he clothe you – O you of little faith!' (Luke 12:27,28).

What do you want to say to God right now? Perhaps a prayer inspired by your flower? Or maybe you want to thank God for some good thing which has blossomed in your life?

Take a moment to reflect, then we'll go around the group and pray our prayers out loud. As we do so, let's each place our flower into the vase.

Petals templates

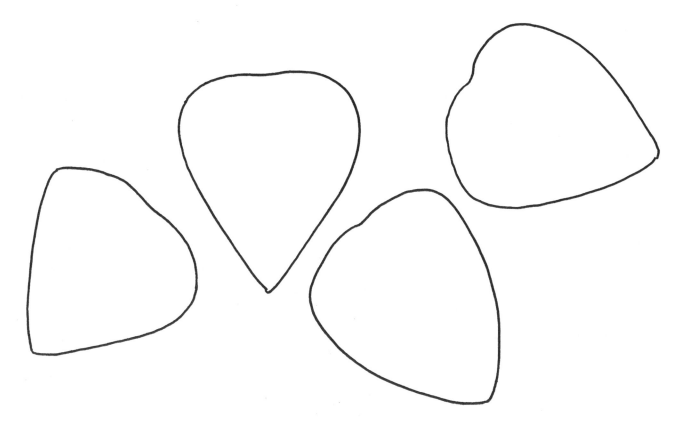

FACTFILE: The Good Shepherd

A shepherd had to walk long distances over difficult terrain, so he had to travel light. These are the items a well-equipped shepherd might carry:

✓ **cloak**: woollen cloth or sheepskin

✓ **water flask**: made from pottery or a hollowed gourd

✓ **scrip**: a bag containing his food (bread, cheese, dried fruit, olives)

✓ **horn of oil**: for treating the wounds of an injured sheep

✓ **staff**: a long stick used for guiding the sheep

✓ **rod**: a club for defence against robbers and wild animals – heavy at one end, with a leather cord at the other so it could be suspended from the shepherd's belt

✓ **sling**: a weapon for hurling stones at an attacker; a skilful shepherd might also sling a stone in front of a sheep that was beginning to stray

✓ **pipe**: a musical instrument similar to a recorder

8 Party people

Luke 14:15–24

The parable of the great banquet

When a well heeled host gave a smart dinner party, it was the custom to issue two invitations. The first went out before the big day; the second was dispatched once the feast was ready. To accept the first invitation and then decline the second was counted a shameful discourtesy.

Jesus was dining with a prominent Pharisee when one of the assembled guests made a pious observation: 'Blessed are those who will eat at the feast in the kingdom of God.' He had in mind the promise of Isaiah 25:6: '…the LORD Almighty will prepare a feast of rich food for all peoples…' But the Old Testament prophecy was merely God's first invitation, and now Jesus had come to call the people to take their places: 'The time has come …The kingdom of God is near. Repent and believe the good news!' (Mark 1:15). The parable of the great banquet is indeed glorious good news. We are saved not by our own efforts but through God's gracious invitation. But it also stands as a solemn warning to those who would snub his call.

Note: Why not run this session in conjunction with a meal? Use the ideas for **Getting connected** while you serve a starter or nibbles; the main course can accompany **Living Scripture**; the **Touching God** activity incorporates dessert; discuss the suggestions for **Reaching out** over coffee and mints. Two or three volunteers might like to get together to prepare the food.

 Getting connected (Starter or nibbles)

Either

Guest of honour

Q: If you could invite a famous guest to your party – either an historical figure, a fictional character, or a current celebrity – who would you choose and why? Discuss your answers around the group.

Or

Party food

This is a game you can play around the table. The first player begins, 'I went to a party and I ate asparagus' (or any other food beginning with the letter 'A'). The next person repeats the sentence, including the 'A' word, and adds a 'B' word (for example, 'I went to a party and I ate asparagus and blancmange'). Try to keep going until you have completed the alphabet.

Or

Taste test

You will need: several bowls of potato crisps or other nibbles – as many different flavours as you can find – and with each bowl numbered; paper and pencils.

Distribute pens and paper and get tasting. See who can identify the most flavours correctly.

 Living Scripture – Luke 14:15–24 (Main course)

You will need: copies of the place mat on page 38.

Read the passage together before you serve the main course. Respond to the questions as you eat.

1 Why do you think Jesus compared the kingdom of God to a party?

2 The servant delivers the invitation to three groups of people: those who had been invited (verse 17); the poor, the crippled, the blind and the lame (verse 21: note that physical disability was often taken to be punishment from God as a consequence of sin); those in the roads and country lanes (verse 23). Who do you think the different groups represent?

3 Jesus told this story while he was dining with a prominent Pharisee. How might his host have reacted?

4 Did the invited guests offer valid excuses for not coming to the banquet (verses 18–20)? What excuses do people give today for refusing Jesus' invitation?

5 How does this parable challenge your priorities?

6 Why is this story such good news?

 ## Touching God (Dessert)

Prayer cake

You will need: a cake; birthday cake candles and holders, enough for one each.

Place the cake in the centre of the table and give everyone a candle and holder. Take it in turns to light your candle and thank God for something that has encouraged or challenged you during your discussion, or pray for someone you know who has not yet accepted Jesus' invitation. Then add your candle to the cake.

When everyone has prayed, read Isaiah 25:6–9 together from your place mats. Finally, blow out the candles and enjoy dessert!

 ## Reaching out (Coffee and mints)

Food for the hungry

Discuss the ways in which you could support people who do not have enough to eat. Could you organise a fundraising event and send the proceeds to an aid agency such as World Vision or Christian Aid? Is there a local project working among the homeless in your area? How could you help? Decide on a suitable project and make plans.

 ## Digging deeper

Give each member of the group a copy of bookmark 8 on page 75 to take home.

A feast of rich food

On this mountain the LORD Almighty will prepare
a feast of rich food for all peoples,
a banquet of aged wine –
    the best of meats and the finest of wines.
On this mountain he will destroy
the shroud that enfolds all peoples,
the sheet that covers all nations;
    he will swallow up death for ever.
The Sovereign LORD will wipe away the tears
    from all faces;
He will remove the disgrace of his people
    from all the earth.
        The LORD has spoken.
In that day they will say,
'Surely this is our God;
    We trusted in him, and he saved us.
This is the LORD, we trusted in him;
    let us rejoice and be glad in his salvation.'

Isaiah 25:6–9

The parable of the great banquet

When one of those at the table with him heard this, he said to Jesus, 'Blessed is the man who will eat at the feast in the kingdom of God.'

Jesus replied, 'A certain man was preparing a great banquet and invited many guests. At the time of the banquet he sent his servant to tell those who had been invited, 'Come, for everything is now ready.'

But they all alike began to make excuses. The first said, 'I have just bought a field and I must go and see it. Please excuse me.'

Another said, 'I have just bought five yoke of oxen, and I'm on my way to try them out. Please excuse me.'

Still another said, 'I have just got married, so I can't come.'

The servant came back and reported this to his master. Then the owner of the house became angry and ordered his servant, 'Go quickly into the streets and alleys of the town and bring in the poor, the crippled, the blind and the lame.'

'Sir,' the servant said, 'what you ordered has been done, but there is still room.'

Then the master told his servant, 'Go out to the roads and country lanes and make them come in, so that my house will be full. I tell you, not one of those men who were invited will get a taste of my banquet.'

Luke 14:15–24

9 Shepherd's delight

Luke 15:1–10

The parables of the lost sheep and the lost coin

Jesus insisted on partying with all the wrong people – at least, that's how it seemed to the Pharisees and teachers of the law. They had a saying, 'There will be joy in heaven over one sinner who is obliterated.' Jesus challenged their misguided notion with his picture of a shepherd on a rescue mission, searching the crags and crevices for a lost sheep, and then his delight at finding the poor, bewildered creature.

A second story concerns a woman searching the house for a missing coin which might have been given to her as part of a necklace or headdress on her wedding day. Once again, the tale has a happy ending.

The Old Testament Scriptures are woven through with images of sheep and shepherds. Again and again, in song and in prophecy, God is seen as a shepherd to his people. Jesus claimed the picture and made it a metaphor for himself: 'I am the good shepherd; I know my sheep and my sheep know me … and I lay down my life for the sheep' (John 10:14,15).

 Getting connected

Lost property
Q: Have you ever lost something that was precious to you? What steps did you take to try to get it back? Share your experiences in the group.

 Touching God

Either

Good shepherd
You will need: copies of the **Good Shepherd factfile** on page 35; flip chart pad or a roll of white lining paper; white card; pencils; black felt-tip pens; scissors; string; sticky tape; stapler; glue sticks; a sound effect of bleating sheep (sound effects are available on CD from some of the larger music shops, or search the Internet for a free download) or background music.

Encourage everyone to choose an item from the **Good Shepherd factfile** and to make a simple representation of it using the craft materials – either a simple cut-out shape or a three-dimensional replica. It does not matter if some people select the same item. Allow 10-15 minutes. Play the music or sound effect (set to repeat) while you work.

When you are finished, lay out your artefacts, or use them to 'dress up' a member of the group. Read John 10:14,15, then take two or three minutes in silence while you simply look at what you have made. How do these objects help you appreciate Jesus, the Good Shepherd? Share your thoughts and let them lead you into prayer and praise.

Finish by reading or singing a version of Psalm 23. If someone can play the recorder they could use their 'shepherd's pipe' to accompany the singing!

Or

Psalm 23 revisited

You will need: copies of **Psalm 23 revisited** on page 42.

Begin by reading or singing a version of Psalm 23 together.

Give everyone a copy of the sheet and ask them to rewrite the psalm by filling in the blanks, replacing the image of a shepherd with a different occupation. Work alone or in pairs. Read out this example to help people get the idea:

> The Lord is my *motor mechanic*,
> I shall not *be abandoned on bricks in a lay-by*.
> He makes me *run even in the winter weather*,
> He leads me *in for retuning; he refuels my tank*.
> He guides me *down safe roads* for his name's sake.
> Even though I *steer through a contraflow in the rush hour*,
> I will fear no *collision*, for you are with me;
> Your *traffic cones* and your *recovery truck*, they comfort me.
> You *wash and wax my bodywork* in the presence of my enemies.
> You *anoint my tappets with oil*; my *sump overflows*.
> Surely your goodness and love will follow me all the days of my life,
> And I will *dwell in the garage* of the Lord for ever.

Finally, read out your psalms to each other.

 ## Living Scripture – Luke 15:1–10

1 Who do you think the shepherd and the woman represent? In Jewish society neither shepherds nor women were highly regarded, so why do you think Jesus chose them for his central characters?

2 Who do you think the ninety-nine sheep and the nine coins represent? Read Isaiah 53:6. In the light of this verse, what do you make of Jesus' comment about 'ninety-nine righteous persons who do not need to repent' (verse 7)?

3 Who do you think the lost sheep and the missing coin represent? What efforts do the shepherd (verses 3–5) and the woman (verse 8) make to find them? Make a list of all the significant 'action' words in these verses. What do they suggest about God's attitude to sinners?

4 When have you been aware of God searching for you, bearing you on his shoulders, or rejoicing over you?

5 Does your church focus on the lost or on the 'ninety-nine'? What are you doing to reach out to those who are lost? How could you be more effective in evangelism?

Reaching out

Either

Faith survey

You will need: copies of the **Faith survey** on page 43.

Give everyone two copies of the survey and encourage them to find two friends who do not attend church who are willing to answer the questions. Pray that God will lead everyone to the right people. If anyone is intrigued by the questions, you could invite them to a group meeting. If they respond positively to Question 8, it may be the right moment to share the gospel with them – but be sensitive!

Bring the answers back to your next meeting and look at them together in the **Reaching out** time. Remember your promise to keep the identity of the people a secret. What have you learned that could help you become better at reaching out?

Or

Friends

You will need: several lengths of knitting wool, 25-30 cm long (optional).

Read out the following:

> Jesus went out of his way to spend time with 'sinners' and befriend them (Luke 15:2).
>
> Around 80 per cent of people who come to faith in Christ do so through their relationships with Christians.
>
> There is a story about a woman who met the Victorian statesmen, Gladstone and Disraeli. Asked to compare them, she said, 'After an evening in the company of Mr Disraeli, I felt he was the most fascinating man in the world. After an evening with Mr Gladstone, I felt I was the most fascinating woman in the world.'
>
> The best way to make new friends is to become genuinely interested in other people.

Pause for one minute to reflect, then pray together, asking God to help you turn at least one acquaintance into a friend by showing an interest in them this week. When you have finished praying, tie a length of wool around each other's wrists as a reminder. Come next time ready to talk about how you got on.

Digging deeper

Give each member of the group a copy of bookmark 9 on page 75 to take home.

Psalm 23 revisited

The Lord is my_____, I shall not_____.

He makes me_____,

He leads me_____, he_____.

He guides me_____ for his name's sake.

Even though I_____,

I will fear no_____, for you are with me;

Your_____ and your_____, they comfort me.

You_____ in the presence of my enemies.

You_____; my_____.

Surely your goodness and love will follow me all the days of my life,

And I will_____ of the Lord for ever.

artist / builder / chef / computer programmer / nurse / fireman / fitness instructor / gardener /
motor mechanic / refuse collector / ship's captain / school teacher

Faith survey

a) Begin by reading out the following:

'I am part of a group which meets to study the Bible. We are conducting a survey into contemporary thinking about the Christian faith. The survey is anonymous; your answers may be discussed in the group, but your name will not be revealed.'

b) Ask the questions and write down the answers. If the answer is more than a simple 'yes' or 'no', read back what you have written to check that you have recorded it accurately. Do not be tempted to defend your point of view – listen and learn!

1 Why do you think people don't go to church?

_____

2 Do you believe in God?

_____

3 Do you ever pray?

_____

4 Would you call yourself a Christian?

_____

5 Who do you think Jesus Christ was?

_____

6 What do you think happens to us when we die?

_____

7 Do you think God is interested in you personally?

_____

8 If it were possible to know God as a friend, would you be interested?

_____

c) Thank the person for their help.

10 Missing persons

Luke 15:11–32

The parable of the lost son

There is a Buddhist fable about a waster of a son who comes to his senses and heads for home. On his return, his father hides and orders the servants to test the boy to discover whether he is truly penitent. Only when the son has endured a series of arduous trials does the father receive him back.

Jesus' parable of the lost son depicts a very different sort of father. It was not unknown for a man to hand over the running of the family estate before his death, but the younger son in Jesus' story demands his share in hard cash, and he wants it now. He might just as well have said, 'I wish you were dead!' His pleasure is short-lived – he soon reaches rock bottom and makes for home, planning to beg employment as a hired hand; but he is little more than a speck in the distance when his father casts all dignity aside and rushes out to welcome him. He clothes him in the best robe (a symbol of status) and gives him a signet ring (a sign of authority). He puts sandals on his feet, as only a slave would go barefoot. Jesus presents us with an astonishing and heart-warming picture of the love of God.

But don't forget: this is the story of *two* sons, and both – in their different ways – are far from the father.

 Getting connected

Either

Pass the Pigs

You will need: *Pass the Pigs* game (manufactured by MB Games).

Play a round of *Pass the Pigs*. Award a prize for the first person to reach the target score.

Or

Home and away

Q: How old were you when you left home? Where did you go? Share your experiences in the group.

Or

Shoddy job

Q: What was the worst job you were ever paid to do?

 Touching God

Either

Rembrandt

You will need: copies of the painting *The Return of the Prodigal Son* by Rembrandt van Rijn. Rembrandt produced several paintings based on the parable. The most famous, the one displayed in the State Hermitage, St Petersburg, is easy to find on the Internet and reproductions are often available in Christian bookshops. An earlier picture, an etching in the collection at the Rembrandt House Museum, Amsterdam, is less well known, but perfect for this activity. Type 'Rembrandt prodigal son etching' into your Internet search engine.

Allow five minutes for people to look at the picture without talking. Then share any observations or insights. Let your conversation lead you into prayer.

Or

Family ties
You will need: a ball of string.

Stand together in a circle. One person has the ball of string. They begin by praying a short prayer of thanksgiving for someone else in the group; for example, 'I thank God for Jo because... ' or, 'I see the love of God in Sam because... ' Everyone joins in with an 'Amen.' The person with the string then holds onto the end and throws the ball across to the person they have named. That person repeats the process, giving thanks for another member of the group. They also hold onto the string, looping it around a finger, and throw the ball across the circle. With each new prayer, the web grows. Try to keep the string taut and continue until everyone has been included at least once. Finish by reading Ephesians 3:14–19 before you let go of the string.

 Living Scripture – Luke 15:11–32

You will need: copies of the cartoon strip on page 47; copies of the script on pages 48 and 49; lively instrumental music to suggest a party (optional).

Give everyone a copy of the cartoon strip. Recruit five volunteers to read the script on pages 48 and 49, taking the following roles: Jesus; younger son; father; servant; elder son. If you have background music, introduce it at the point indicated.

1 Who were the first people to hear the parable of the lost son (see Luke 15:1,2)? In the light of this, who would you say the following characters in the story represent: the father; the younger son; the older son?

2 Why do you think the younger son asked for his share of the estate (verse 12)? Why did the father agree to his request?

3 What does it take to bring the younger son 'to his senses' (verse 17)? Was there ever a time when God acted to bring you back to your senses?

4 What do you notice about the father's welcome to his son in verses 20–24? What is the significance of the robe, the ring and the sandals? (See the session introduction.) What do these verses convey about the character of God?

5 Why is the elder brother so angry (verses 28–30)? Do you sympathise with his point of view? In what way is he also 'lost' even though he never left home?

6 Turn to the cartoon strip. Which picture best represents your life at the moment? Take two or three minutes in silence to reflect, and then go round the group and share your thoughts. Break into small groups of three or four people to pray for each other.

Reaching out

Either

Heavenly hug

Which of your family and friends is most in need of a 'hug' from their heavenly Father right now? Is there a picture in the cartoon strip that reflects their struggle? Pray for them.

Or

Art exhibition

Organise an art exhibition based on the **Digging deeper** activity. Perhaps you could join forces with other groups using the same material and display your work in the church, local community centre, or public library. Design a leaflet to explain the exhibition and, if possible, have people on hand to answer questions. You could extend the idea by running a competition for local artists based on the parable and award prizes at a church service where the story of the lost son is the theme.

 Digging deeper

Give each member of the group a copy of bookmark 10 on page 75 to take home.

The parable of the lost son

Script: The parable of the lost son

Jesus	Once there was a man who had two sons. One day his younger son came to him.
Younger son	Father, give me my share of the property – right now.
Jesus	So the man divided his wealth between them. A few days later the younger son converted his share into hard cash, and left home. He journeyed to a far distant country where he squandered the money in madcap living until he had frittered away every last penny.
	Not long afterwards, a terrible famine spread throughout the land. The younger son was left destitute. Eventually he found work with a local landowner who sent him into the fields to feed pigs. He would have been glad to fill his belly with the bean pods the pigs were given, but no one gave him anything. The pigs were eating better than he was! At long last, he came to his senses.
Younger son	My father's labourers have plenty to eat, and here I am starving to death! I'll go back to my father, and say to him, 'Father, I've been a fool. I've sinned against God and against you. I'm no longer fit to be called your son but, I beg you – take me back as one of your hired workers.'
Jesus	The younger son started on his long journey home. He was no more than a speck in the distance when his father saw him approaching. The old man's heart was filled with compassion and he ran out along the road. He flung his arms around his son and kissed him.
Younger son	Father, I've been a fool. I've sinned against God and against you. I'm no longer fit to be called your son…
Jesus	But the father called out to his servants.
Father	Quick! Bring a robe, the best you can find, and shoes for his feet. Put a ring on his finger. Slaughter the prize calf and prepare a feast. Let's party! My son was dead, but now he is alive. He was lost, but now he is found.

[*Introduce the background music. It continues throughout the remaining dialogue.*]

Jesus	And so the festivities began. Meanwhile, the elder son was working in the fields. As he was nearing home he heard music and dancing. He questioned one of the servants.
Elder son	What's going on here?
Servant	Your brother has come home. He's back – alive and well – and your father has called for a celebration. We've even killed the prize calf!
Jesus	The elder son was angry and refused to go into the house. His father came out and begged him, but still he wouldn't budge.
Elder son	All these years I have slaved for you and never let you down. When did you ever give me even a goat so I could celebrate with my friends? This son of yours has squandered your money on prostitutes and wild living. He comes home, and now you're killing the prize calf for a big celebration!
Father	My son, you are always here with me, and everything I have is yours. But don't you see, we have to celebrate? Your brother was dead and now he is alive again. He was lost but now he's found.

11 All worked up

Matthew 19:23 – 20:16

The parable of the workers in the vineyard

The scene was a familiar one. Throughout the region, the grapes were ripe and ready to harvest. They had to be gathered quickly before the autumn rains came, so the local landowner would be in the marketplace at the crack of dawn, looking for workers to bring in his crop. The going rate was one denarius for a day's work – a modest wage that did not allow for luxuries. Life for these men was a hand to mouth affair, and a day without work meant the whole family would go hungry.

The unfamiliar twist in Jesus' tale is that the landowner returns to enlarge his workforce, not once but *three* times, and then insists on paying the last of the hired men a whole day's wages. His startling generosity provokes a storm of protest. But this is a parable, and Jesus needs his disciples to understand that the kingdom of heaven does not operate by worldly wisdom.

 Getting connected

Either

Not fair
Q: When have you ever been stirred to say, 'It's not fair'? For example, have you ever taken part in a protest march, or been on strike, or written to your MP? Share your experiences.

Or

Amazing grace
Q: When did someone last give you more than you deserved?

 Touching God

Either

Taste and see
You will need: a basket of grapes.

Use Psalm 34 to praise God, using the script on pages 54 and 55. One person holds the basket of grapes and reads Psalm 34:1,2. Everyone else responds by saying together, 'Taste and see that the Lord is good' (verse 8a). Meanwhile, the first person eats a grape and hands the basket on to the next person, and so on. After reading their part, each person eats a grape and passes them on. Try to keep the psalm flowing.

Or

Golden grapes
You will need: the template on page 53; several sheets of gold or yellow card; two plant sticks; a 4 cm square of flexible card; paper punch; gold or yellow parcel string or wool; scissors; pens.

A feature of the temple in Jerusalem was a magnificent ornamental vine, with grapes of solid gold, which surrounded the entrance to the Holy Place. It was considered an honour to give gold, so more fruit could be added. Contributions were sometimes made in gratitude to God for a blessing received.

Create a group mobile inspired by the golden vine. Make the support structure before the meeting. Punch four holes in the card square and thread through the plant sticks in a X-shape, making the four arms of equal length. Attach a loop of string around the sticks at the point where they touch so that you can hang up your mobile. Use the template to cut out several 'bunches of grapes' from gold or yellow card. You will need two or three for each person. Punch a single hole at the top of each bunch.

Share out the grapes. Take four or five minutes in silence to think back over recent weeks and bring to mind the good things you have received from God. Write simple prayers of thanksgiving on the grapes. Invite everyone to share what they have written.

Now assemble your mobile. Take each bunch of grapes and thread a loop of string through the hole. Suspend the grapes from the plant sticks, varying the length of each string so the grapes hang at different heights. Adjust their position along the sticks until the mobile is balanced.

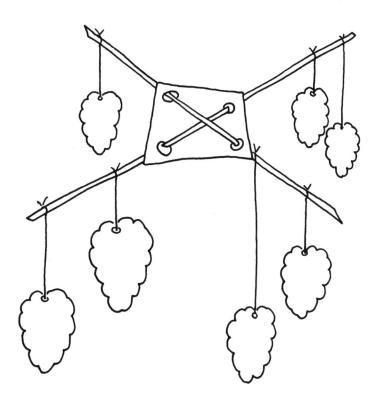

Or

Golden grapes/alternative
Instead of turning your prayers into a mobile, you could simply attach the golden grapes to a door frame with Blu-tack, or tie them to the branches of a large twig fixed upright in a pot.

 Living Scripture – Matthew 19:23 – 20:16

You will need: grapes to share while you discuss the questions (optional).

Recruit five volunteers to read the following roles in the passage: narrator; disciple (19:25); Jesus/landowner; Peter (19:27)/the grumbling worker (20:12); hired worker (20:7). Tackle the questions together after the reading.

1   If the landowner in the parable represents God, who do the hired workers represent?

2   Why does Jesus tell this story to the disciples? What have they failed to understand (see 19:23–30)?

3   Why does the landowner bother to hire additional workers for the last hour? What motivates him to pay a whole day's wages for one hour's work? What does this suggest about the character of God?

4   'Friend, I am not being unfair to you,' said the landowner (20:13). Do you agree? What, if anything, do you think the denarius represents?

5   Read Luke 23:32–43. How does Jesus' promise to the penitent thief shed light on the meaning of the parable?

6   Read Romans 6:23 and Ephesians 2:8,9. Are you ever tempted to think of salvation as a reward for services rendered, rather than a gift of grace? What is God saying to you through this parable? Take a few minutes in silence for reflection then pray for one another in twos or threes.

 Reaching out

Either

The last will be first
Who do you know who has recently come to faith in Christ, or who is on the brink of faith? How could you reach out to support and honour them? For example, could you invite them to the group, or offer lifts or babysitting so they can attend church? Could you send a gift from the group – perhaps a helpful book – with a note assuring them of your prayers?

Or

Fair trade feast
Organise a group social event where you serve a meal prepared, as far as possible, from fairly traded goods. Invite people from outside the group to join you. Alternatively, plan a more ambitious event to raise awareness of trade justice issues in your church or local community. Produce a written menu with notes about the ingredients; invite a guest speaker or organise an informative quiz; have a stall of fairly traded goods for sale. Sell tickets – charging a realistic price to cover the cost of the food. You could send any profits on to an aid agency which works to alleviate the effects of poverty. Type 'Fairtrade Foundation' into your Internet search engine for further information and links. Decide on a plan of action and share out the tasks.

 Digging deeper

Give each member of the group a copy of bookmark 11 on page 76 to take home.

Template for a bunch of grapes

Parable charades

A lamp under a bowl	The lost son	The shrewd manager
The fig tree	The net	The talents
The friend at midnight	The pearl	The tenants in the vineyard
The good Samaritan	The persistent widow	The ten bridesmaids
The great banquet	The rich fool	The unmerciful servant
The hidden treasure	The rich man and Lazarus	The weeds
The lost coin	The sower	New wine in old wineskins
The lost sheep	The sheep and the goats	The wise and foolish builders

Script: Taste and see

First person: I will extol the LORD at all times;
his praise will always be on my lips.
My soul will boast in the LORD;
let the afflicted hear and rejoice.

All: Taste and see that the LORD is good.

Second person: Glorify the LORD with me:
let us exalt his name together.
I sought the LORD, and he answered me;
he delivered me from all my fears.

All: Taste and see that the LORD is good.

Third person: Those who look to him are radiant;
Their faces are never covered with shame.
This poor man called, and the LORD heard him;
he saved him out of all his troubles.

All: Taste and see that the LORD is good.

Fourth person: The angel of the LORD encamps around those who fear him,
And he delivers them.
Taste and see that the LORD is good;
blessed is the man who takes refuge in him.

All: Taste and see that the LORD is good.

Fifth person: Fear the LORD, you his saints,
for those who fear him lack nothing.
The lions may grow weak and hungry,
but those who seek the LORD lack no good thing.

All: Taste and see that the LORD is good.

Sixth person:	Come, my children, listen to me; I will teach you the fear of the LORD. Whoever of you loves life and desires to see many good days, Keep your tongue from evil And your lips from speaking lies. Turn from evil and do good; Seek peace and pursue it.
All:	Taste and see that the LORD is good.
Seventh person:	The eyes of the LORD are on the righteous and his ears are attentive to their cry; the face of the LORD is against those who do evil, to cut off the memory of them from the earth. The righteous cry out, and the LORD hears them; He delivers them from all their troubles.
All:	Taste and see that the LORD is good.
Eighth person:	The LORD is close to the broken-hearted and saves those who are crushed in spirit. A righteous man may have many troubles, but the LORD delivers him from them all; he protects all his bones, not one of them will be broken.
All:	Taste and see that the LORD is good.
Ninth person:	Evil will slay the wicked; the foes of the righteous will be condemned. The LORD redeems his servants; no-one will be condemned who takes refuge in him.
All:	Taste and see that the LORD is good.

12 Grape expectations

Mark 11:27 – 12:12

The parable of the tenants in the vineyard

The grapevine had become a symbol for Israel. The great golden vine that surrounded the entrance to the Holy Place was one of the glories of the temple, and it was probably in view as Jesus told his story about a vineyard and a gang of callous tenant farmers. No one could have been in any doubt – the parable was meant as a picture of Israel's history.

It was also meant as autobiography. Jesus had been accosted by a group of officials wanting to know the source of his authority. He spoke of a beloved son, sent by the owner of the vineyard in a last-ditch effort to win over his tenants. The son is brutally murdered and his body left to rot. Within three days of telling the story, Jesus himself had been crucified.

But Jesus concludes with a play on words, a promise that death will not be the end. The word for 'son' in both Hebrew and Aramaic is *ben*, while *eben* is the word for a 'stone'. He quotes Psalm 118:22,23: 'The stone the builders rejected has become the capstone.' Jesus, not Israel, is the true vine, and the source of all life and growth.

 Getting connected

Either

Fresh fruit salad
You will need: an assortment of fresh fruit; apple juice or orange juice; single cream (optional); utensils for cutting, peeling and serving.

Work together to prepare a fruit salad. Share out the jobs and get into pairs to chat about your week as you work. Serve the fruit salad during the **Reaching out** part of the meeting.

Or

Growing up
Q: Did you have a garden to play in when you were a child? What do you remember about it? Share your memories in the group.

 Living Scripture – Mark 11:27 – 12:12

You will need: a large sheet of paper; marker pen.

Recruit three volunteers to read the following parts: narrator; questioner (11:28,31–33); Jesus. After the reading, pray that God will speak to you through one another as you explore the passage, and then tackle the questions together.

1 Read Isaiah 5:1–7. What similarities do you notice between the 'Song of the Vineyard' and the parable? List them in the top left hand corner of your sheet. The passage from Isaiah would have been very familiar to the chief priests, the teachers of the law and the elders who first heard Jesus' story. What conclusions would they have drawn about the vineyard, the owner, and the tenants?

2 Read Jeremiah 7:25,26. Who do the servants in the parable represent? Write your answer in the top right hand corner of your sheet. How does the ill-treatment of the servants go from bad to worse (12:2–5)?

3 Read Mark 1:9–11. What does Jesus say about his identity and his mission through this parable? Write any insights in the bottom left hand corner of the sheet.

4 Read John 15:1–8. What message does the story contain for Christians today? How does it encourage or challenge you? Write your thoughts in the bottom right hand corner of the sheet.

 ## Touching God

Either

Cross examined

You will need: the paper from **Living Scripture**; a cross, about 75 cm tall, constructed from rough wood and fixed upright in a large plant pot or bucket by surrounding it with stones; copies of the prayers on page 59; a tray of red poster paint; a bucket of water; soap and a towel; appropriate background music, for example Samuel Barber's *Adagio for Strings* (optional).

Put the paper flat on the floor and stand the cross in the centre. Begin with a moment of silence and look again at what you have written. Give out the sheets and say the prayers together. Pause where indicated to cover the cross with your handprints. You may want to play a piece of instrumental music in the background as you do this. When you come to the washing, do this in silence, one by one, and listen to the splashing of water. Don't hurry.

Or

Cross examined/alternative

Instead of using a wooden cross, you could simply make handprints directly onto the paper. Work together in silence to build up the shape of a cross in the space between the words.

Or

Holy Communion

Join together in a simple celebration of Communion. Use the large sheet of paper from **Living Scripture** as a table covering and set out the bread and wine on top. Different churches have different practices, so check with your minister; if your tradition only allows an ordained priest to celebrate Communion, you may be able to use bread and wine which have already been consecrated in a church service.

 ## Reaching out

Either

Garden party

Who do you know who would appreciate help with a garden or allotment – perhaps a friend who has recently moved house, or a neighbour who is elderly or unwell? Or do you know of a public garden in need of attention, for example: the land around your church building? Organise a working party. You could combine your efforts with a social event such as a barbecue or afternoon tea.

Or

The fruit of the Spirit is love
Do you know someone who is struggling with disappointment or rejection? Pray for them. Make plans to send a fruit cake or an attractive basket of fruit to let them know they are loved. Include a card with a message of encouragement.

 Digging deeper

Give each member of the group a copy of bookmark 12 on page 76 to take home.

Prayers: Cross examined

Leader: He had one left to send:
a son, whom he loved.

All: But they took him and killed him,
and threw him out of the vineyard.

Take it in turns to press your hands into the paint and cover the cross with your handprints.

Leader: Let us admit our sins to God.

All: Lord God, we have sinned against you.
We have resisted your Word and rejected your Son.
Have mercy on us according to your unfailing love.
Wash away our wrongdoing and cleanse us from our sin,
through Christ, our Saviour. Amen.

Keep silence as each person washes the paint from their hands. When everyone is clean:

Leader: Jesus said, 'You are already clean because of the word I have spoken to you. Remain in me as I also remain in you.'

An opportunity for anyone to pray. Thank God for the cross in your own words.

Leader: The stone the builders rejected has become the cornerstone;

All: The Lord has done this, and it is marvellous in our eyes.

Leader: Jesus is the true vine.

All: And we are the branches.

Leader No branch can bear fruit by itself.

All: Neither can we bear fruit unless we remain in him.

Leader: Every branch that does bear fruit the Father prunes,
so that it will be even more fruitful.

All: This is to our Father's glory, that we bear much fruit,
showing ourselves to be his disciples.

13 Ready or not

Matthew 25:1–13

The parable of the ten bridesmaids

A wedding was a great event. The celebrations began when the bridegroom arrived to claim his bride and lead her through the village streets to his family home. The torchlit procession would take the longest possible route, so that as many people as possible had the chance to wish them well. Following the ceremony, the couple kept open house for a week. They were treated like royalty, and sometimes even wore crowns and special robes. In a peasant society where life was hard, their week of feasting and fun was a big occasion for the whole community. But, with so much to prepare, it could sometimes be a long time before the bridegroom showed up and, in the parable of the ten bridesmaids, half the bridal party are caught by surprise with tragic consequences.

 Getting connected

Either

Comic timing

Q: Are you usually a latecomer or an early bird? Think back to a time when you turned up very late or very early for an event, with amusing consequences. What happened? Share your experiences.

Or

Parable charades

You will need: a hat or other container; photocopies of parable titles from page 53 cut up into slips of paper.

Divide into two teams and play charades against the clock. Someone from Team A takes a slip of paper. They must communicate the parable to their teammates without speaking, either by acting out the whole story, or by dividing the title into separate words or syllables. When the team has guessed correctly, a second player collects a new slip of paper and takes over. Continue for four minutes before switching to Team B. After two or three rounds, count up how many parables each team managed to identify in the time.

Or

Music factory

You will need: assorted tins, plastic containers and any other kitchenware such as pots or wooden spoons suitable for making percussion instruments; dried pulses or rice.

Work together to make instruments for the **Percussion praise** activity (see **Touching God** below). Shakers can be improvised from tins or plastic containers with well-fitting lids. Fill them about a quarter full with rice or dried peas. A pair of wooden spoons banged together make good rhythm sticks. A plastic bucket, turned upside down, can become a hand drum. Experiment to find other objects which make a satisfying sound when knocked or rattled.

Touching God

Either

Percussion praise

You will need: percussion instruments (see **Music factory** above).

Appoint someone to be the leader of your band. You will also need one or two people to read.

The band leader sets up a four-beat rhythm and everyone else joins in. Practise getting louder or quieter, following the leader. When you have got the hang of playing together, the reader can join in with **The Song of the Bride** (Isaiah 61:10,11) below, speaking rhythmically to fit with the music. If you have two readers, they can speak out alternate lines.

The Song of the Bride

I delight greatly in the LORD,

my soul rejoices in my God.

For he has clothed me with garments of salvation

and arrayed me in a robe of righteousness,

as a bridegroom adorns his head like a priest,

as a bride adorns herself with her jewels.

(Band quieter)

As the soil makes the young plant come up

and a garden causes seeds to grow,

(Band louder)

so the Sovereign LORD will make righteousness and praise

spring up before all na-tions.

Glory to the Father, and to the Son,

and to the Holy Spi-rit,

as it was in the beginning, and is now

and shall be for ever. A-men.

Or

Haiku praise-poems

You will need: writing paper; copies of the instructions on page 64; background music such as *In Paradisum* from Fauré's *Requiem* (optional).

Give out the instructions and read them through together. Allow 10-15 minutes for people to compose their *haiku*, either working alone or in pairs; then share the results. You could play a piece of gentle music in the background as you read your poems.

 Living Scripture – Matthew 25:1–13

Recruit volunteers to read the following parts in the story: Jesus/bridegroom; wedding guest (verse 6); foolish bridesmaid; wise bridesmaid. After the reading, work through the questions together.

1 What did Jesus mean by 'that time' (verse 1)? (Think about the focus of his teaching throughout Matthew 24 and 25.)

2 What is the difference between the wise and foolish virgins? Why did the wise virgins refuse to share their oil? What warnings does the parable contain?

3 It is plain that the bridegroom represents Jesus himself (compare Matthew 9:14,15). What does the image convey to you about his love for the world? Why would a loving God 'shut the door' on anyone?

4 'Therefore keep watch, because you do not know the day or the hour' (verse 13). If you knew the Second Coming was scheduled for tomorrow, what would you do today? Take two or three minutes in silence to reflect, then share your thoughts.

5 How does the promise of Christ's return affect the way you live? What part of your discussion has challenged or encouraged you the most? Break into threes or fours and pray for each other.

 Reaching out

Either

Scatter the darkness

You will need: a heat resistant surface such as a tray filled with sand; a large candle; tea lights; background music (optional) – this could be the same as for the *haiku* activity.

Set the candle in the centre of the tray and light it. Dim the lighting in the room, if possible, and pray by candlelight.

'I tell you the truth, I don't know you' (verse 12). If Jesus were to return tomorrow, who among your family and friends would be caught unprepared? Take two or three minutes to pray for them in silence. You might like to play some quiet instrumental music in the background as you do so.

Pass the tea lights around the group and encourage everyone to take one for each of the people they have prayed for. Take it in turns to light them from the central candle and place them in the tray. As you do so, name the person you have prayed for. When all the tea lights are lit, the leader prays:

God our Redeemer, you sent Jesus to be the Light of the World. Stir the hearts of our friends and family members, and kindle in them a love for you so that, together, we may be ready to greet him when he comes again. Amen.

Or

Wedding party

Plan a special event for all the couples who have been married at your church during the last five years. For example, you could invite them to a short service with prayers for marriage and family life, or provide a buffet meal followed by a talk from an expert on communication or managing the family budget. Discuss the possibilities and decide on a plan of action.

 Digging deeper

Give each member of the group a copy of bookmark 13 on page 76 to take home.

Haiku praise-poems

Haiku is a Japanese form of poetry where each poem has just three lines. The first line has five syllables, the second seven, and the third five. *Haiku* often express far more than would seem possible in just a few words. It is not essential to stick to the pattern of 5-7-5 syllables, but aim to write short lines where every word counts. If you wish, you can also add a title.

Here are some examples and titles to get you started.

Holy Trinity
Source of all being;
Saviour and Eternal Word;
Breath of life within.

The wisdom of God
Love beyond reason:
See your creator, stripped and
nailed to two rough planks.

Revelation
Eyes like blazing fire;
Beauty shining like the sun:
The First and the Last.

Suggested titles for your own *haiku* praise-poems:

Blessing / Bridegroom / Creation / Daily bread / Faith, hope, love / Father God / Good shepherd / Holy Spirit / Kingdom of heaven / King Jesus / Light of the world / Peace / Prayer / Resurrection / Saviour of the world / Still small voice / Thanksgiving / Walking on water / Your kingdom come

14 Active service

Matthew 25:14–30

The parable of the talents

When we meet someone with a flair for music, art or mathematics, we describe them as 'talented'. Originally, though, a 'talent' was a unit of weight, equivalent to about 30 kilograms. One talent of gold would amount to 15 years' wages, while five talents was more than most labourers could earn in a lifetime. The word took on its popular meaning from this parable, in which Jesus uses gold as a metaphor for the wonderful variety of opportunities, resources and spiritual insight which God has entrusted to his people. The story promises great blessing for those who use them bravely, but the master's anger falls on the third servant who is too fearful or lazy to take a risk.

Note: If you choose the **Godly Play** and **Hidden Talents** activities, some advance preparation is needed.

 Getting connected

Worthy cause

Q: If you were given a large sum of money to invest in a worthy cause or project, what would you use it for? Share your ideas with one another.

 Living Scripture – Matthew 25:14–30

Either

Godly play

You will need: a piece of green felt, about 80 cm by 50 cm; a strip of brown felt, about 80 cm by 10 cm; a small box containing 15 coins of identical value (pound coins if you can afford them!); the four figures on page 70 copied onto card, coloured and cut out; an attractive box to contain all the above.

This activity is based on 'Godly play' techniques which were developed to help young children engage with God through the Scriptures. They offer a refreshing way into the Bible for adults too. You will need to learn the script off by heart. Practise telling the story with the materials until you are confident. (If this approach appeals to you, there are scripts and figures for other parables in *Young Children and Worship* by Sonja Stewart and Jerome Berryman (published by Westminster/John Knox Press, US), the originators of 'Godly play'. With a little thought, they can be adapted for use with adults.)

Have the group sit in a circle, preferably on the floor. Before you introduce the materials, explain that you are using a storytelling technique devised for use with children which will include some 'I wonder… ' questions. Young children usually speak out the thoughts that occur to them, so encourage everyone to behave like children and respond in the same way!

Take the green felt from the box and follow the script on pages 68 and 69.

Or

Questions

Recruit five volunteers to read the story, taking the following roles: Jesus; first servant; master; second servant; third servant. After the reading, discuss the questions.

1. In the story, who do the master and the three servants represent? What could the bags of gold represent? You may be able to list a number of possibilities. Why do you think the three servants receive different amounts of gold (verse 15)?

2. What do you notice about the response of the first two servants (verses 16,17)? What does this suggest about their relationship with the master? How does the master reward them on his return (verses 21,23)?

3. Why does the third servant hide his bag of gold instead of putting it to use (verses 24,25)? What does this suggest about his relationship with the master? Why is the master so hard on him (verses 26–30)?

4. How does the master remind you of God? In what ways is he different?

5. Jesus originally meant the parable as a challenge to the people of his own day. How would they have interpreted verses 28,29? How has the parable encouraged or challenged you?

 Touching God

Either

Creative talents

You will need: an assortment of art and craft materials such as paper, card, tissue paper, old magazines, scrap fabric, colouring pencils, felt-tip pens, glue sticks, adhesive tape, stapler, scissors, wool or string, garden wire, plant sticks, gold and silver foil, modelling clay or play dough; background music (optional).

What do you want to say to God after considering the parable? Encourage everyone to make a personal response using the art and craft materials: either a picture, a collage, or a piece of sculpture. Others might prefer to compose a poem or piece of creative writing. Allow about 15 minutes. Try not to talk but pray silently as you work. You might want to play some appropriate instrumental music in the background.

When time is up, share what you have made. If you chose the **Godly play** option, let the insights which emerged lead you into discussion.

Or

Hidden talents

You will need: (for the preparation session) luggage labels; a hat or other container; (for the worship activity) inexpensive gifts with written prayers attached.

Prepare a week in advance. Each person writes their name on a luggage label and drops it into a hat. Then everyone draws out one, checking that they have not picked out their own name. Agree a modest spending limit that everyone can afford. During the week, make or buy a present for the person whose name you have selected: try to find something which represents a God-given gift or talent that you appreciate in them. Wrap the gift, then write a prayer for the person on the back of their luggage label and attach this to the gift. Bring it along to the meeting.

Collect the gifts and redistribute them without revealing the identity of the givers, but do not give them to the person whose name is on the label at this stage. Go around the group and read out the written prayers. After each prayer, hand the package to the appropriate person.

Reaching out

Either

Cash challenge

Each member of the group begins with £5 or £10 and aims to double it (or more!) in support of a mission organisation or charity. For example, you could use the money to buy ingredients and make cakes for sale; or buy craft materials, envelopes, etc and produce greetings cards. Some members may prefer to combine their resources and work with a partner.

Or

Giving time

Pray for friends or family members you would love to introduce to Jesus Christ. Give time to them this week (paying a visit, writing a letter, making a phone call), and ask God to give you an opportunity to share something of your faith.

Digging deeper

Give each member of the group a copy of bookmark 14 on page 76 to take home.

Godly play script

First, we need a background. *(Spread out the green felt. From now on, focus entirely on the story-telling materials and avoid making eye-contact with people. This will feel strange at first, but it is a powerful way of drawing everyone into the story.)* It is green. I wonder what the colour green reminds you of...?

(Handle the materials with care, as though they are precious. Build up the scene, upside down as you look at it. Place the brown felt along the bottom edge of the background to represent a strip of ground, then place the master at one side with his feet on the ground.)

Jesus said: The kingdom of heaven will be like a man ... *(point to the man)* ... going on a journey. He called in his servants ... *(take out the other three figures and place them in a row, first the butler, then the cook, then the gardener)* ... and entrusted his wealth to them.

Hidden coin

Green felt

Brown felt

To one he gave five bags of gold ... *(take out five coins and place them in a column above the head of the butler)* ... to another two bags *(place two coins above the cook)* ... and to another, one bag ... *(place one coin above the gardener)* ... each according to their ability. Then he went on his journey ... *(slide the master along and hide him under the background, out of sight)*.

The servant who had received five bags of gold went at once and put his money to work, and gained five bags more ... *(place a second column of five coins above the butler)* ... so also, the one with two bags of gold gained two more *(place two more coins above the cook)* ... but the man who had received one bag went off, dug a hole in the ground and hid his master's money ... *(take the gardener's coin and 'bury' it under the brown strip)*.

After a long time the master of those servants returned and settled accounts with them ... *(return the master to his starting position)* ... the servant who had received five bags of gold brought the other five. 'Master,' he said, 'you entrusted me with five bags of gold. See, I have gained five more.' His master replied, 'Well done, good and faithful servant! You have been faithful with a few things; I will put you in charge of many things. Come and share your master's happiness!'

(Swap over the master and the butler, and move ten coins to be over the butler's head. The master should now be next to the cook.)

The servant with the two bags of gold also came. 'Master, you entrusted me with two bags of gold: see, I have gained two more.' The master replied, 'Well done, good and faithful servant! You have been faithful with a few things; I will put you in charge of many things. Come and share your master's happiness!'

(Swap over the master and the cook, and move four coins to be over the cook's head. The master should now be next to the gardener.)

Then the one who had received the one bag of gold came. 'Master,' he said, 'I knew that you are a hard man, harvesting where you have not sown and gathering where you have not scattered seed. So I was afraid and went out and hid your gold in the ground. See, here is what belongs to you.'

(Retrieve the one coin from under the brown strip and place it back over the gardener's head.)

His master replied, 'You wicked, lazy servant! So you knew that I harvest where I have not sown and gather where I have not scattered seed? Well then, you should have put my money on deposit with the bankers, so that when I returned I would have received it back with interest. The bag of gold will be taken from you and given to the one who has ten bags … *(add the gardener's coin to the butler's ten)* … For those who have will be given more, and they will have an abundance. As for those who do not have, even what they have will be taken from them. Throw that worthless servant outside, into the darkness, where there will be weeping and gnashing of teeth!'

(Remove the gardener from the background and place him on the floor, just to one side. Allow a moment for everyone to take in the scene, then continue with the 'I wonder…' questions. Keep your eyes on the story. Respond to each suggestion simply by affirming it, repeating the answer, or simply saying, 'Yes.')

I wonder … how this person … *(point to the gardener)* … is feeling right now?

I wonder … how this person … *(point to the master)* … is feeling?

I wonder … who the master in the story could stand for?

I wonder … who the servants in the story really are?

I wonder … what the gold could be?

I wonder … why the master gave this person five bags of gold … and this person only two bags?

I wonder … why the third servant hid the gold instead of putting it to use?

I wonder … why the master was so hard on the third servant?

I wonder … what we can learn from this story?

At the end, carefully return all the items to the box and close the lid as a sign that the story is completed.

15 Long division

Luke 16:19–31

The parable of the rich man and Lazarus

The contrast between them could not be more stark: a rich man enjoying the very best in designer clothing and opulent living; his destitute neighbour, too sick and weak even to fend off the street dogs that torment him. The poor beggar is the only character in any of the parables to whom Jesus gave a name – *Lazarus*, meaning 'God is my help'. We see the promise of his name fulfilled in the next scene. Both men have now died; Lazarus is in heaven while the rich man must endure all the miseries of hell. Jesus based his description on contemporary ideas about the 'geography' of the afterlife, and it would probably be a mistake to take it too literally. But the point is clear – the choices we make in this life affect our eternal destiny.

 Getting connected

Meeting in heaven

Q: Who do you look forward to meeting in heaven? What question do you want to ask them? Share your responses.

 Touching God

Either

Resurrection snap

You will need: photocopied cards using the template on page 73; uplifting background music: *The Lark Ascending* by Ralph Vaughan Williams would be a good choice.

Shuffle and deal out the 16 *Resurrection Snap* cards. Someone with a *Dead?* card reads it aloud and places it in the centre of the group. The person with the most appropriate *Alive!* card then responds by reading it and placing it on top. Continue in this way until you have matched up all the pairs. Finally, pray together, thanking God for the resurrection of Jesus and all that it means for us.

Or

Resurrection art

You will need: copies of the painting *The Incredulity of St Thomas* (Neues Palais, Potsdam) by Caravaggio, or *The Supper at Emmaus* (National Gallery, London) by the same artist. Both pictures are available via the Internet. Or choose a different work of art based on an encounter with the risen Jesus.

Make sure everyone can see a copy. Allow four or five minutes for people to look at the picture, then share any observations or insights. Let your conversation lead you into praise.

 Living Scripture – Luke 16:19–31

You will need: a version of Charles Dickens' *A Christmas Carol* on DVD or video for question 5 (optional).

Recruit volunteers to read the following parts of the passage: Jesus (narrator); rich man; Abraham. After the reading, work through the questions together.

1 What details does Jesus include to stress the prosperity and poverty of the two neighbours (verses 19–21)? If you were retelling the parable with contemporary characters, what details would you include to emphasise the differences between them?

2 Why didn't the rich man help Lazarus? Why do people neglect the poor today?

3 Jesus' vivid description of heaven and hell (verses 22–26) was based on the popular thinking of the times. How far should it be taken literally? What essential truths about the afterlife does the parable convey?

4 Does getting into heaven depend on the way we treat others in this life?

5 If you are using the movie, show the scene where Marley's ghost appears to Scrooge. Why doesn't God really send messengers from the dead to persuade people to repent (verses 27–31)?

6 How has this parable challenged you? Break into threes or fours to share your thoughts and pray for one another.

 ## Reaching out

Either

Goat games night
Plan a fund-raising event to buy a goat for a poor African family. You can do this through an agency such as *Farm Africa* or *Christian Aid*. Devise goat-related games such as 'pin the tail on the goat', a 'goat drive' (like a beetle drive), or 'goat skittles' (made from plastic bottles). Include a goat-related quiz. Ask everyone to make a contribution each time they play a game, and award prizes. Invite friends from outside the group to join you.

Or

Prayer walk
Go out in groups of two or three on a 'prayer walk' around the local area. Imagine Jesus to be walking with you and try to see the people and places with his eyes. What needs do you notice? Stop to pray from time to time. Come back together after 15-20 minutes and discuss what you observed. How can you reach out and make a difference?

 ## Digging deeper

Give each member of the group a copy of bookmark 15 on page 76 to take home.

Resurrection snap

Dead?
Jesus didn't really die on the cross. He fainted and later recovered in the cool of the tomb.

Alive!
Jesus had been flogged, crucified, and stabbed with a spear. His dead body was sealed in a tomb and left to rot. It is inconceivable that he could have 'come round' and escaped in a fit state to convince everyone that he had overcome death!

Dead?
It was still dark when the women discovered the empty tomb. In their distress and confusion, they had got the wrong place!

Alive!
Daylight would soon have revealed their mistake. The disciples, guards or Jewish leaders would have pointed out the truth immediately.

Dead?
The Jewish authorities removed the body because they were afraid the disciples would steal it and start the rumour that Jesus had risen from the dead.

Alive!
If the Jewish leaders had taken the body, they could easily have produced it to scotch the Christians' claim.

Dead?
Jesus' body was removed by the Romans. They did not want the tomb to become the focus for civil unrest and rebellion.

Alive!
If the Romans had the body, why didn't they produce it when rumours of Jesus' resurrection began to fly?

Dead?
The disciples stole the body themselves and started the rumour that Jesus had risen from the dead.

Alive!
Why would they? All the disciples' hopes were dashed when Jesus was crucified. It took a miracle to transform them into the revolutionary group we read about in Acts. Most suffered punishment and even death for their faith. Would they really have done all that for a hoax?

Dead?
Grave robbers must have raided the tomb and stolen Jesus' body.

Alive!
Why would anyone steal a dead body? The only things of value in the tomb were the grave clothes, and they were left behind! What's more, thieves would have had to get past the Roman guard.

Dead?
The disciples sincerely believed they had seen Jesus alive, but they were hallucinating.

Alive!
The disciples were not expecting to see Jesus again, and yet he appeared to them on at least 11 occasions over six weeks. He was seen by more than 550 people including Saul (later Paul) who was a fierce enemy of the first Christians. The risen Christ was no hallucination!

Dead?
Jesus did not rise from the dead. What the eyewitnesses saw was a ghost.

Alive!
The disciples touched him, felt the wounds in his hands and side, walked and talked with him. On one occasion he even cooked breakfast for them. The risen Jesus was no ghost!

5 Love actually

Aim to do something kind for someone every day this week. You could put a sticking plaster around your finger as a reminder. Pray that God will present you with opportunities for practical love and service. Remember that Christ called us to love difficult people as well as those we find it easy to love (Luke 6:32–35). Let these verses on the theme of love encourage you:

Day 1 1 John 4:7,8
Day 2 1 John 4:9,10
Day 3 1 John 4:11,12
Day 4 1 John 4:16–18
Day 5 1 John 4:19,20
Day 6 1 John 4:21

4 Pass it on

What do you learn from each of these passages about **forgiveness**? If you can, as you read and reflect, hold three large nails in your hand to remind you of the price Jesus paid for our forgiveness.

Day 1 Mark 2:1–12
Day 2 John 8:2–11
Day 3 Luke 23:26–37
Day 4 Luke 23:39–49
Day 5 Matthew 26:69–75; John 21:15–19
Day 6 Romans 8:1,2

3 Finders keepers

Picture postcards: Buy six inspiring picture postcards and write out Matthew 13:44–46 on the back of each one. Leave them in unlikely places for others to find.

And/or

Pearl of great value: Write an autobiographical short story, poem, or 'letter to the future' about your relationship with Christ. Give it the title *Pearl of great value*. Begin with Matthew 13:44–46.

And/or

Prayer cache: Make a note of all the concerns you bring to God in prayer this week. Seal your list in an envelope (with this bookmark as a reminder) and put it away somewhere safe. Make a note in your diary or on your calendar to remind you to re-open the envelope at a later date – say in six months or a year – when you can thank God for any prayers that have been answered or pray again for anything still unresolved.

2 Firm foundations

Read through the Sermon on the Mount. Look for a command to obey each day, and take a few minutes to memorise it. You may want to carry a pebble in your pocket to remind you of it through the day.

Remember Take a few moments to get comfortable and remember that God is with you. Pray that your heart will be receptive, like good soil.

Read the passage through.

Day 1 Matthew 5:1–16
Day 2 Matthew 5:17–32
Day 3 Matthew 5:33–48
Day 4 Matthew 6:1–18
Day 5 Matthew 6:19–34
Day 6 Matthew 7:1–23

1 Arable parable

Set aside time to reflect on the following passages this week, using an ancient way of praying known as *lectio divina* or 'godly reading'. Don't be discouraged if it feels awkward to begin with; you will get better with practice.

Remember Take a few moments to get comfortable and remember that God is with you. Pray that your heart will be receptive, like good soil.

Read the passage through.

Day 1 Isaiah 55:10,11
Day 2 Mark 4:26–29
Day 3 Luke 10:2
Day 4 Matthew 13:31,32
Day 5 John 4:35–37
Day 6 1 Corinthians 3:6–9

Reflect Re-read the passage again, slowly. When a word or phrase catches your attention, savour it. Allow it to fill your thoughts. Don't hurry. Feeding on the Scriptures like this was sometimes compared to an old cow quietly chewing its cud!

Respond Let your reflections lead you into prayer. What do you need to say to God? What is God wanting to say to you?

Rest When you run out of words, don't rush away. Enjoy sitting still in the presence of God.

6 Breadtime story

Focus on one section of the Lord's Prayer each day; then read the 'door verse', and let the questions lead you into prayer.

Day 1 Father, hallowed be your name; Psalm 100:4. How many different names for God can you think of?

Day 2 Your kingdom come; Revelation 3:20. How has God been 'locked out' by the world or the Church? Pray for two or three specific situations.

Day 3 Give us each day our daily bread; Luke 11:10. What gift do you need from your loving and generous Father today?

Day 4 Forgive us our sins; John 10:9. Remember the ways you have sinned against God, and pray for forgiveness.

Day 5 For we also forgive everyone who sins against us; Psalm 141:3. Ask God to help you forgive those who have hurt you, and to give you grace in dealing with the people you find difficult.

Day 6 And lead us not into temptation; Genesis 4.7. Name the things you find it hard to resist. Pray that the Holy Spirit will give you the strength and discipline to overcome temptation. Remember that the death of Christ has overcome the power of evil.

7 A fool and his money

Re-read Luke 12:24–26, then take 15–20 minutes to sit quietly and watch the birds in your garden or local park. What do you learn from their activity?

And/or

Study these six passages about our attitude towards material wealth:

Day 1 Matthew 19:16–24
Day 2 Mark 12:41–44
Day 3 Luke 16:19–31
Day 4 2 Corinthians 9:6–15
Day 5 1 Timothy 6:6–10
Day 6 1 John 3:16–18

8 Party people

There are more mealtime scenes in Luke than in any of the other gospels. Set aside time over breakfast or lunch to explore the following passages. As you read, look out for: (1) something savoury: a challenging verse you can chew over; (2) something sweet: a mouth-watering promise!

Day 1 Luke 5:27–39
Day 2 Luke 7:36–50
Day 3 Luke 11:37–54
Day 4 Luke 14:1–14
Day 5 Luke19:1–10
Day 6 Luke 22:7–38

9 Shepherd's delight

If possible, go for a walk in the country this week. Take your Bible and stop in sight of a field of sheep, or in 'green pastures', or 'beside quiet waters'. Choose one of the following passages and let it speak to you. You might like to join together with one or two other members of your group and take a picnic.

If you can't get out of an urban environment, why not visit a local park? Sit on a bench and let your imagination get to work!

Day 1 Psalm 23 or Psalm 100
Day 2 Isaiah 40:10,11
Day 3 Ezekiel 34:11–23
Day 4 John 10:1–10
Day 5 John 10:11–21
Day 6 John 21:15–17

10 Missing persons

The parable of the lost son has inspired a great many artists (for example, Rembrandt), writers (such as Dickens) and composers (including Debussy, Prokofiev, Britten). Create your own 'work of art' based on the parable. Pray that God will take you deeper into the story as you work. Here are some suggestions:

Pictures: abstract or figurative; use pencil or paintbrush; or produce a collage using material from newspapers or magazines; or use a camera to create a series of photographs based on the story; or work with fabric and appliqué.

Sculpture: use modelling clay or scrap materials.

Written word: choose a character and tell the story from their perspective, or write a poem; try to get inside thoughts and feelings; perhaps transfer the action to a modern day setting.

Drama: write a play script to be performed by people or puppets; or make a set of masks which could be used by actors to tell the story in mime.

Music/dance: compose a song or a piece of instrumental music; perhaps you could develop a dance to go with your composition.

11 All worked up

These verses all reflect the way in which the kingdom of heaven turns worldly wisdom on its head. Take time to meditate on them this week. You might like to combine your reflection with the activity: Work into worship.

Day 1 Mark 9:35
Day 2 Matthew 18:3,4
Day 3 Luke 9:24
Day 4 1 Corinthians 1:18
Day 5 1 Corinthians 1:25
Day 6 Isaiah 55:9

Work into worship: Choose a household chore or a routine part of your paid work, and turn it into worship. For example, if you are preparing a meal, prepare it as though you are cooking for Jesus himself; if you are setting the table or making the bed, do it as though Jesus is a guest in your home. Let the activity remind you of aspects of God's character.

12 Grape expectations

Enjoy a piece of fruit as you reflect on these verses. Eat slowly and chew on the words.

Day 1 Genesis 3:2,3: Not all fruit is good for us; some berries are poisonous. What temptations do you struggle to resist? Pray for strength.

Day 2 Leviticus 19:23–25: Fruit does not grow and ripen overnight. Are you waiting for an answer to prayer? Pray for patience.

Day 3 Matthew 7:16,17: Is your faith in Christ obvious to others? Pray that your conduct will honour God.

Day 4 John 15:1,2: What needs pruning in your life? How is your Father calling you to cooperate with him?

Day 5 Galatians 5:22,23: Where do you feel weakest? Ask the Holy Spirit to help you grow and mature in that area.

Day 6 Hebrews 13:15: What do you want to praise God for today?

13 Ready or not

What do you learn from these passages about wisdom? Make a note of anything you discover.

Day 1 Proverbs 3:13–24
Day 2 2 Chronicles 1:1–12
Day 3 1 Kings 3:16–28
Day 4 Luke 20:20–26
Day 5 John 8:1–11
Day 6 1 Corinthians 1:18–31

At the end of the week, compose an acrostic poem on the theme of wisdom. Here is an example based on Proverbs 3:13–24.

Worth

Immeasurably more than

Silver or gold.

Do not let me

Out of your sight.

My name is Wisdom.

14 Active service

'Repent and be baptised … and you will receive the gift of the Holy Spirit' (Acts 2:38). The Holy Spirit has been given to equip us for service. It is important to remember that the Holy Spirit is God's personal presence, not just a 'force'. But the Bible often refers to the Spirit through metaphor and symbol. Reflect on the following verses. You might like to use objects or pictures as a focus for your prayers. There are suggestions below, but you may be able to think of others. Add a new item each day. Pray for an increase of the Holy Spirit's power in your life.

Day 1 Genesis 1:1,2; John 1:32,33 (a white feather)

Day 2 Acts 2:1,2; John 3:8 (a model sailing boat)

Day 3 Acts 2:3,4; Matthew 3:11 (a lighted candle)

Day 4 Isaiah 44:3; John 7:37–39 (a glass of water)

Day 5 1 Samuel 16:13; Mark 6:12,13 (a container of olive oil)

Day 6 Luke 11:11–13; 1 Corinthians 12:4–7 (gifts from the *Hidden talents* activity)

15 Long division

Day 1 Matthew 13:24–30; 36–43
Day 2 Matthew 13:47–52
Day 3 Matthew 25:31–46
Day 4 Revelation 1:9–20
Day 5 Revelation 4
Day 6 Revelation 22

Perhaps you could draw or paint a picture based on the passages from Revelation. Or read *The Great Divorce* by C S Lewis (quite a short novel, around 100 pages) about a bus which travels between hell and heaven. What do you find in the story to inspire and challenge you?

Other books in the Multi-Sensory series

✳ fresh   ✳ innovative   ✳ imaginative   ✳ inspirational   ✳ practical

MULTI-SENSORY CHURCH

Over 30 ready-to-use ideas for creative churches and small groups

Sue Wallace

This invaluable resource includes a variety of ways of exploring the senses to expand your understanding and grow your delight in prayer, liturgy, Bible reading, celebration, labyrinths and much more.

MULTI-SENSORY PRAYER

Over 60 ready-to-use ideas for creative churches and small groups

Sue Wallace

Ways to use the senses to enrich your prayer experience – using everything from candles and broken pottery to nuts, leaves, newspapers, dough and mirrors!

MULTI-SENSORY SCRIPTURE

50 innovative ideas for exploring the Bible in churches and small groups

Sue Wallace

Bible-focused ideas to expand understanding and grow delight in many aspects of confession, intercession, meditation and much more.

MULTI-SENSORY SEASONS

15 ready-to-use Bible-based sessions through the seasons for creative small groups

Wendy Rayner and Annie Slade

Complete small group sessions based on a range of Biblical material from both Old and New Testaments that can be used any time or tied to a specific season of the church calendar.

MULTI-SENSORY TOGETHER

15 ready-to-use sessions for Bible exploration in creative small groups

Ian Birkinshaw

15 complete sessions for leaders which will breathe new life into small group Bible study experience. Will appeal to a range of learning styles. Based on biblical material from both Old and New Testaments.

COMING SOON!   **Multi-Sensory Prophets**

Also about parables…

Parabulz invites younger readers to explore parables in the Bible, both Old and New Testaments. 112 pages of retold story, explanation, poems, cartoons, fact boxes – to help readers tease out what the original storyteller was wanting to communicate.

Zany illustrations by **Andy Gray** enhance this easy-to-read book by **Andrew Bianchi**.

Parabulz is a fun read for 8-11s – but also a refreshing accompaniment for anyone using *Multi-Sensory Parables*. And an inspirational resource for anyone involved in ministry.

Also for small groups...

the Word made fresh! is a series of lively and relevant discussion starters for small groups wanting to think about biblical principles as they affect and challenge contemporary life. Ideal for new or established groups of 6-14 members with limited or extensive Bible knowledge, who prefer a fairly unstructured programme. Each title contains ten sessions of thought-provoking input from Stephen Gaukroger, senior pastor of one of the UK's largest mainstream churches, plus worksheets.

Revival Living

insights from 1 Timothy for the 3rd millennium church

Transition Living

insights from 1 Samuel for the 3rd millennium church

A Code for Living

the Ten Commandments for the 3rd millennium church